N
E

D0763627

For Reference

Not to be taken from this room

HIPPOCRENE CONCISE DICTIONARY

NEPALI-ENGLISH ENGLISH-NEPALI DICTIONARY

PRAKASH A. RAJ

HIPPOCRENE BOOKS
New York

For information, write:
HIPPOCRENE BOOKS, INC.
171 Madison Avenue
New York, NY 10016

CONTENTS - Basaya suchi

Nepali Language

Nepali is the national language of the kingdom of Nepal and is also spoken in parts of northeast India and Bhutan. It belongs to Indo-European family of languages and is closely related to Hindi and north Indian languages. As is **Devanagari** script which is supposed to be phonetic.

The pronunciation as given in this dictionary is as follows:

a	as	in	maroon
aa	as	in	father
i	as	in	rich
ee	as	in	peace
u	as	in	should
oo	as	in	moore
o	as	in	core
e	as	in	best
ai	as	in	paying
au	as	in	fowl
am	as	in	dumb

How to read Nepali **(Devanagari)** alphabet ?

Vowels

a अ   aa आ   i इ   ee ई   u उ   oo ऊ
e ए   ai ऐ   o ओ   au औ   am अं

Consonants

ka क	kha ख	ga ग	gha घ	nga ङ
cha च	chha छ	ja ज	jha झ	yan ञ
ta ट	tha ठ	da ड	dha ढ	ana ण
ta त	tha थ	da द	dha ध	na न
pa प	pha फ	ba ब	bha भ	ma म
ya य	ra र	la ल	wa व	
sha श	sha ष	sa स	ha ह	
ksha क्ष	tra त्र	gya ज्ञ		

Certain sounds in Nepali alphabet such as bha, chha, jha and dha have no equivalent in English. Similarly such letters as f and sh have no equivalent sounds in Nepali (spoken) although they are used in the written language.

The emphasis on preparing this dictionary is on words which are in day-to day use rather than Nepali as used in newspapers and books which is heavily sanskritized as it contains many words borrowed from Sanskrit.

Nepali Numerals

1	2	3	4	5	6
Ek	Dui	Teen	Chaar	Paanch	Chha

7	8	9	10	0
Saat	Aath	Nau	Das	Sunya

20	30	40	50	60
Bees	Tees	Chaalees	Pachaas	Saathi

70	80	90	100
Sattari	Assi	Nabbe	Saya

NEPALI-ENGLISH

aabashyak / adj. essential
aadar / n. respect
aadha / adj. half
aadhaar / n. basis
aadhunik / adj. modern
aankha / n. eye
aagaami / in the future
aago / n. fire
aagya / n. order
aagyaakaari / adj. obedient
aahaar / n. food
aahaari / one who take food
aaja / adv. today
aaja raati / adv. tonight
aakarshan / n. attraction
aakaash / n. sky
aakhir / n. end
aakhiri / adj. final
aalu / n. potato
aalubakhada / n. plum
aamaa / n. mother

aamaa baabu / n. parents
aandhi / n. storm
aandolan / n. unrest; movement
aangan / n. courtyard
aandraa / n. intestine
aanp / n. mango
aansu / n. tear
aapasi / adj. mutual
aapat / n. disaster
aaphu / oneself
aaraam / n. rest
aarogya / n. health
aarthik / adj. financial
aascharya / n. surprise
aashaa / n. hope
aashaa garnu / v. to hope
aatmaa / n. soul
aattinu / v. to get nervous
aath /eight
aaunu / v. to come
aawaaj / n. sound

aayog / n. board
aayojana / n. scheme; project
aayu / n. age
aba / adv. now
aba dekhi / from now on
abasar / n. occasion
abelaa / n. late
abhyaas / n. practice
abhaagi / adj. unlucky
abhimaan / n. arrogance
abhimaani / adj. arrogant
achamba / n. surprise
achaanak / adj. all of a sudden
adaalat / n. court
addaa / n. office
adhikaar / adv. right
adhuro / half done
adhyaksha / n. chief; chairman
aduwa / n. ginger
agaadi / adv. ahead; before
ageno / n. fireplace

aghaaunu / v. to be filled up with food

aghi / adv. before; in front of

ahile / adv. at the moment; right now

ahile dekhi / from now on

ajha / adv. still; yet

akmakaaunu / v. to hesitate

aksar / adv. frequently; often

akshar / n. letter of alphabet

alag / adj. separate

alchhi / adj. lazy

alikati / adj. a little

almalinu / v. to be puzzled

amar / adj. immortal

ambaa / n. guava

amilo / adj. sour

andaa / n. egg

andaaj garnu / v. to guess

andaaji / adv. approximately

anibarya / adj. compulsory

andho / adj. blind

andhakaar / n. darkness

angaalo / n. embrace
angrez / n. Englishman
angrezi / n. English
ani / conj. and then
anikaal / n. famine
anna / n. food grain
anmol / adj. valuable
antar / n. difference
antar-rashtriya / adj. international
antim / n. last
anubaad / n. translation
anubhab / n. experience
anuchit / adj. improper
anuhaar / n. appearance
anumaan / n. estimate
anumati / n. permission
anurodh / n. request
anusandhaan / n. research; investigation
anusar / adj. according to
anushasan / n. discipline
anyaya / n. injustice

apach / n. indigestion
apamaan / n. insult
aparaadh / n. crime
aparaadhi / n. criminal
araaunu / v. to order
arko / adj. another; next
artha / n. finance, meaning
aru / adj. more
asadhya / n. incurable
asajilo / adj. difficult
asal / adj. good
asali / adj. genuine, real
asambhab / adj. impossible
asankhya / adj. innumberable
asaphal / n. failure
asaar / name of a month in Nepali calendar
asar / n. effect
assi / eighty
asti / day before yesterday
astra / n. weapon
atankabaadi / n. terrorist

ater / adj. disobedient
ati / adj. excessive, extreme
atmaa / n. soul
au / cong. and
aulo / n. malaria
aupachaarik / adj. official
aunthi / n. finger ring
aushadhalaya / n. medicine store
aushadhi / n. medicine
ausat / n. average
awasthaa / n. situation; condition
ayogya / adj. unfit
baa / n. father
baabu / n. father
baachaa / n. promise
baachchho / n. calf
baachnu / v. live
baadal / n. cloud
baadhaa / n. obstruction
baadhyataa / n. compulsion
baadhnu / v. tie

baadi / n. plaintiff
baagh / n. tiger
baahek / prep. except
baahira / n. outside
baahiriyaa / n. outsider
baahun / n. brahmin
baaisi / n. twenty two kingdoms in far western Nepal before 18th century
baaja / n. musical instrument
baaje / n. grandfather
baajhnu / v. quarrel
bajaute / adj. quarrelsome
baaji / n. competition
baakas / n. box
baaklo / adj. thick
baakayaa / n. remainder
baakya / n. sentence
baalaghar / n. home for children
baalak / n. boy
baali / n. crop
baalig / n. adult

baalika / n. girl

baampudke / adj. dwarf

baanchnu / n. survive

baaluwaa / n. sand

baandar / n.monkey

baani / n. habit

baanijya / n. commerce

baango / adj. crooked; bent

baanki / n. leftover, remainder

baansuri / n. flute

baanta / n. vomit

baaph / n. steam

baar / n. day of week, fence

baaremaa / prep. about; concerning

baari / n. garden

baarta / n. talk

baarud / n. artillery

baas / n. lodging for night

baasnaa / n. smell

baastabik / adj. true; authentic

baastabmaa / in fact

baata / prep. from
baataabaran / n. environment
baatho / adj. clever
baato / n. road
baatulo / adj. round
baayan / adv. left
baayu / n. air
baayusewa / n. airline
baayumandal / n. atmosphere
badaam / n. almond
badalaa / n. revenge
badalaa linu / v. revenge
badalnu / v. change
badmaas / adj. bad person
badmaasi / n. misconduct
badnaam / adj.disgraced
bagaichaa / n. garden
bagar / n. rivershore
bagaaunu / v. wash away
bagnu / v. flow
bahaadur / adj. brave

bahaaduri / n. bravery

bahaal / n. rent, monastery

bahar / n. calf

bahas / n. argument

bahini / n. sister

bahiro / adj. deaf

bahiskaar / n. boycott

bahu / adj. many

bahudal / n. multiparty

bahula / adj. insane; mad

bahulatti / n. madness; insanity

bahumat / n. majority

bahumulya / adj. valuable

baikalpik / n. alternate

bains / n. youth

bairi / n. enemy

baisaakh / first month of Nepali calendar

bajaar / n. market

bajaaunu / v. to play an instrument

bajnu / v. play

bakas / n. tip

baknu / v. give testimony

bakulla / n. crane

bakkhu / n. Tibetan jacket

baliyo / adj. strong

balnu / v. burn

bamb / n. bomb

bamojim / prep. according

ban / n. jungle; forest

banaaunu / v. make

banaawati / adj. artificial

banda garnu / v. close

bandargah / n. port

bandhan / n. restriction

bandobasta / n. arrangement

banot / n. shape

banduk / n. gun

banshaj / n. descendant

baraabar / adj. equal

baraph / n. ice

barphi / n. sweet dish

baru / adj. rather

barkhaa / n. rainy season
bartamaan / adj. present
bas / n. bus
bas bisauni / n. bus stop
basaai saraai / n. migration
basant / n. spring
basanti / adj. yellowish color
basnu / v. sit
basti / n. village; settlement
bataaunu / v.explain
batti / n. lamp
bayaan / n. description
bechain / adj. restless
beg / n. speed
beglai / adj. n. separate
behosh / adj. unconscious
behoshi / n. unconsciousness
beimaan / adj. dishonest
beijjat / adj. n. disgrace
bekamma / adj. useless
belaa / n. time; occasion

belukaa / n. evening
bensi / n. lowland
bepaar / n. trade
bepaari / n. trader
ber / adj. late
bernu / v. tie
bes / adv. very good
bessar / n. turmeric
besari / adv. very much
beshyaa / n. prostitute
besi / adv. more
bhaag / n. share; part
bhaagnu / v. run away
bhaagya / n. fate
bhaai / n. brother
bhaale / adj. male animal
bhaalu / n. bear
bhaanjaa / n. nephew
bhaanji / n. niece
bhaansaaghar / n. kitchen
bhaasha / n. language

bhaat / n. cooked rice
bhabishya / n. adj. future
bhabishyabaani / n. forecast
bhabitabya / n. act of God
bhabya / adj. splendid
bhakti / n. devotion
bhandaaphod / n. expose
bhandaa / conj. than
bhaandar / n. store
bhansaar / n. custom
bharyang / n. stairway
bhawan / n. building
bhayaanak / adj. dangerous,; terrifying
bhedaa / n. sheep
bheed / n. rush, crowd
bhelaa / n. gathering
bhesh / n. dress
bhet / n. meeting
bhetghaat / n. meeting
bhetnu / v. meet
bhindi / v. lady's finger (vegetable)

bhitra / adv. within
bhitri / adj. inside
bhog / n. possession
bhok / n. hunger
bhoko / adj. hungry
bholaa / adj. simple, innocent
bholi / adv. tomorrow
bhool / n. mistake
bhoolsudhaar / n. rectification
bhraman / n. travel
bhrasta / adj. corrupt
bhrastaachaar / n. corruption
bhugol / n. geography
bhujaa / n. cooked rice
bhukampa / n. earthquake
bhulnu / v. forget
bhumi / n. land
bhut / n. ghost
bhutpurba / adj. former
bhyaaguto / n. frog
bibidh / adj. different

bichalit / adj. disturbed

bichaar / n. opinion; thinking

bichaar garnu / v. think

bichhaunu / v. spread; lay down

bichchhi / n. scorpion

bichitra / adj. strange

bidaa / n. leave

bidaabaari / n. farewell

bideshi / n. adj. foreigner

bidesh / n. foreign country

bidyaa / n. learning

bidyaalaya / n. school

bidyaarthi / n. student

bidhawaa / n. adj. widow

bidhwamsha / n. adj. destruction

bigaarnu / v. spoil

bigyaan / n. science

bigyaapan / n. advertisement

bihaana / n. morning

bihibaar / n. thursday

bijaya / n. victory

bijuli / n. electricity

bijulighar / n. powerhouse

bikaas / n. development

bikalpa / n. alternative

bikh / n. poison

bikhaalu / adj. poisonous

bikri / n. sale

bikri garnu / v. sell

bikriti / n. deficiency

bilaas / n. luxury

bilkul / a. definitely

bimaa / n. insurance

bimaan / n. aeroplane

bimiro / n. a kind of fruit

binaa / prep. without

binaas / n. destruction

binaya / n. politeness

binti / n. request

bipana / n. state of awakedness

bipakshi / n. opponent

bipareet / adj. opposite

biraha / n. sorrow of separation
birodh / n. opposition
biruddha / prep. against
bisaaunu / v. taking of rest for someone carrying load
bisancho / n. adj. unwell
bishaal / adj. large
bishaya / n. subject
bishesh / adj.n. special
bishista / adj. special
bishraam / n. rest
bishnu / n. hindu deity
bishwa / n. world
bishwaas / n. trust; confidence
biskut / n. biscuit
bisphotak / n. adj. explosive
bistaar / n. extension
bisuddha / n. pure
bistaarai / adv. slowly
bitaran / n. distribution
biteko / adj. past
bitnu / v. pass time; die

bitulo / n. impure

biu / n. seed

bojh / n. weight

bokro / adj, n. peel

boksi / n. witch

brahmaa / n. hindu god of creation

brahmachaari / n. adj. celibate

buddhi / n. wisdom

buddhimaan / n. adj. celibate

budhi / n. old woman

buhaari / n. daughter-in-law

bujhaaunu / v. make understand; entrust

bujhnu / v. understand

burush / n. brush

butta / n. decoration design

bwaaso / n. wolf

byabahaar / n. behaviour

byaabahaarik / adj. n. practical

byabasaaya / n. occupation

byabastha / n. system

byaaj / n. interest

byakta garnu / v. describe
byakti / n. person
byaktigat / adj. personal
byaktitwa / n. personality
byasan / n. habit
byathaa / n. disease
chaadparba / n. festival
chaado / adv. soon
chaahindo / adj. necessary
chaahinna / I don't need it
chaalchalan / n. conduct
chaanchun / adj. very little
chaakar / n. servant
chaakhnu / v. taste food
chaalu / adj. clever, current
chaamal / n. uncooked rice
chaandi / n. silver
chaar / num. four
chaar kune / adj. square
chaaso / n. concern
chaatnu / v. lick

chaayaa / n. dandruff

chadhaaune / v. raise;offer

chadhnu / v. climb

chain / n. happiness

chakka / n. wheel

chakra / n. wheel

chalaani / n. dispatch

challa / n. chicks

chalnu / v. move

chalta purja / adj. active; clever

chamchaa / n. spoon; adj; flatterer (slang)

chamatkaar / n. miracle

chamero / n. bat

chamkanu / v. shine

chamkilo / adj. shining

chanchal / adj. n. restless

chandaa / n. contribution

chandan / n. sandalwood

chankho / adj. clever

chappal / n. slipper

charan / n. feet; cow pasture

charnu / v. graze
charko / adj. loud
charitra / n. character
charpi / n. bathroom
chashmaa / n. glasses
chautaraa / n. platform for resting
chautarphi / adj. all round
cheen / n. china
chelaa / n. disciple, pupil
chepaang / n. a tribe living in the hills
chepto / adj. wide
chestaa / n. attempt
chewaa / n. peek; check
chewaa garnu / v. peek
chhaadaa / adj. unaccompanied
chhaadnu / v. leave
chhalaa / n. leather
chhaanaa / n. roof
chhaap / n. stamp
chhaapaakhaanaa / n. printing press
chhaataa / n. umbrella

chaati / n. breast; chest

chhaayaa / n. shadow

chhahara / n. waterfall

chhakaaunu / v. deceive

charnu / v. scatter

chhal / n. deception

chhalphal / n. discussion

chheu / n. side

chhimeki / adj. n. neighbour

chhoraa / n. son

chhori / n. daughter

chhoto / adj. small

chhunu / v. touch

chhuri / n. knife

chhutkaara / n. riddance

chhutnu / v. be released

chij / n. object; thing

chilaaunu / v. itch

chinjaan / n. acquaintance

chinnu / v. recognize

chiplanu / v. slip

chiplo / adj. slippery

chiso / adj. cold

chitwan / n. an area in southern Nepal famous for wildlife

chitthaa / n. lottery

chitthi / n. letter

chiyaa / n. tea

chok / n. courtyard

chokho / adj. pure; unpolluted

cholo / n. blouse

chor / n. thief

chor bajaar / n. smuggling market

chori / n. theft

chot / n. wound

chucho / adj. pointed

chuhinu / v. leak

chukli / n. complaint

chuknu / v. miss

chun / n. lime

chunnu / v. elect

chunaab / n. election

chumban / n. kiss
chumban garnu / v. kiss
chup / adj. n. silent
churaa / n. bangle; bracelet
churaute / n. group of moslems living in hills of Nepal
churot / n. cigarette
chusnu / v. suck
chyaau / n. mushroom
chyaapnu / v. hold tightly
chyaatnu / v. tear
chyuraa / n. flattened rice
daabi / n. claim
daabi garnu / v. claim
daaduraa / n. measles
daag / n. spot
daahine / adj. right
daaha samskaar / n. cremation
daaijo / n. dowry
daajnu / v. compare
daajo / n. comparison
daaju / n. brother (elder)

daak / n. post

daakaa lagnu / v. commit robbery

daaku / n. robber

daaktar / n. doctor

daal / n. lentil

daalo / n. a kind of basket

daamlo / n. rope for tying cattle

daan / n. gift; donation

daanaa /n. animal feed

daang / n. district in southern Nepal

daando / n. hills

daanphe / n. national bird of Nepal

daant / n. teeth

daaraa / n. teeth

daaraa kitnu / v. be angry

daari / n. beard

daarim / n. pomegranate

daas / n. servant; slave

daata / n. adj. contributor

daauraa / n. firewood

daavaa / n. right

dabaab / n. pressure

dabaaunu / v. exert pressure; quell

dagurnu / v. run

dabba / n. box

dadhnu / v. burn down

dadhelo / n. forest fire

daha / n. pond

daharo / adj. strong

dahi / n. yogurt; curd

daiba / n. destiny

daibi prakop / natural disaster

dailo / n. threshold

dainik / adv. daily

dailo / n. door

dakaar / n. belch

dakarmi / n. mason

dakhal / n. interference

dakhal dinu / v. interfere

dakshin / adj. south

dakshinaa / n. contribution

dal / n. party

dalaal / n. broker

daldal / n. swamp

dallo / adj. round

danak / n. beating

dam / n. asthma

daman / n. oppression

damkal / n. fire brigade

dampati / n. married couple

dandaa / n. stick

dar / n. fear

dard / n. pain

dari / n. mattress

darjaa / n. rank; post

dar laagnu / v. be afraid

darshan / n. visit

darshan bhet / n. royal audience

darshaniya / adj. worth visiting

darshan shastra / n. philosophy

dartaa / n. listing of incoming letters in an office

dasain / n. biggest festival in Nepal

dashaa / n. bad luck

dasnu / v. bite

dastur / n. tradition; custom

dautari / adj. having same age

dayaa / n. kindness; mercy

dayaalu / n. kind

dayaneeya / adj. pitiable

debal / n. temple

dehaanta / n. death

dehaanta hune / v. die

dekhaa parnu / v. be seen

dekhi / prep. from; since

dekhnu / v. see

deraa / n. temporary lodging

desh / n. country

debataa / n. god

debi / n. goddess

dhaago / n. thread

dhaak / n. boasting

dhaak-chhop / n. cover up

dhaan / n. paddy; rice

dhaara / n. tap

dhalnu / v. fall

dhamilo / adj. unclean

dhan / n. wealth

dhani / n. rich

dhansaar / n. granary

dhanga / n. tact; manner

dhanu / n. bow

dhanyabaad / n. thank

dhapaaunu / v. drive away

dharka / n. line

dharma / n. religion

dharma shaastra / n. scriptures

dharma putra / n. adopted son

dharmaatmaa / adj. pious

dharot / n. deposit

dharati / n. land; earth

dhasnu / v. subside; press down

dherai / adj. many

dhikkar / n. curse

dhilo / adj. slow

dhindo / n. dish made from flour popular in the hills of Nepal

dhipi / n. insistence

dhito / n. deposit

dhobi / n. washerman

dhulo / n. dust

dhunu / v. wash

dhungaa / n. stone

didi / n. elder sister

dikka / adj. worried

din / n. day

dinu / v. give

disaa / n. stool

dishaa / n. direction

diunso / n. afternoon

diyo / n. lamp

dobar / adj. twice

doharyaaunu / v. repeat

doko / n. large funnel shaped basket

dori / n. string

dosh / n. blame

dosh lagaaunu / v. blame

dubnu / v. sink

dudh / n. milk

dukh / n. sorrow

dukhi /adj. unhappy

dukhnu / v. pain; ache

dun / n. valley in southern part of Nepal

dungaa / n. boat

durbin / n. telescope

durgandha / n. smell

durlabh / adj. n. not easily obtained

durust / adj. exact; the same

dushman / n. enemy

dushmani / n. enemity

dushta / adj. wicked

dootaabaas /n. embassy

duwai /pron. adv. duwai both

dwaar / n. door

dwaara / prep. adv. through; by

ek / num. one

ekaa deshmaa / once upon a time

ekaaek / adv. suddenly

ekaanta / adj. n. lonely place

ekata / n. unity

eklo / adv. alone

eutaa / one

gaabhnu / v. annex; incorporate

gaadaa / n. bullock cart

gaadhaa / adj. dense

gaadi / n. vehicle

gaagri / n. utensil for carrying water

gaahak / n. customer

gaahro / adj. difficult

gaai / n. cow

gaaine /n. minstrel

gaajar / n. carrot

gaali / n. abuse

gaanaa / n. song

gaanjaa / n. hashish

gaaunu / v. sing

gaayak / n. singer (male)

gaayikaa / n. singer (female)

gadaa / n. one of four weapons in the hands of Bishnu; large stick

gadbad /n. confusion

gaddaar / adj. n. traitor

gaj / n. yard

gaddi / n. throne

gahaanaa / n. ornaments

gahiro / adj. deep

gaindaa / n. rhino

gair sarkaari / non governmental

galnu / v. deteriorate

galti / n. mistake

gamala / n. flower pot

gambhir / adj. n. serious

ganaaunu / v. smell

gandha / n. smell

gangato / n. crab

ganit / n. mathematics

ganjadi / n. adj. hashish addict

gannu / v. count

ganthan / n. talking of absurd things

ganti / n. counting
garam / adj. hot
garba / n. pride
garbhini / n. pregnant woman
garib / n. adj. poor
garibi / n. poverty
garnu / v. do
garungo / adj. heavy
gati / n. speed
gauchar / n. cow pasture
gaaun / n. village
gaaunle / n. villager
gaur / n. thought
gayal / adj. gayal absent
ghachetnu / v. push
ghainto / n. round earthen water pot
ghamanda / adj. pride
ghamandi / adj. n. proud
ghantaa / n. bell
ghanti / n. alarm bell
ghar / n. house

gharaanaa / n. family

gharelu / adj. domestic

gharelu udyog / cottage industry

gharpatti / n. landlord

ghasnu / v. rub

ghatta / n. water mill

ghatana / v. event

ghataaunu / v. decrease

ghati / n. less

ghatiyaa / adj. n. inferior

ghatnu / v. decrease

gheraa / n. circle

ghernu / v. surround

ghin / n. loathing; hatred

ghinlaagdo /adj. loathsome

ghiu / n. ghee

ghoda / n. horse

ghodejaatra / a festival celebrated in Kathmandu Valley in March

ghuincho / n. crowd

ghumnu / v. revolve, wander

ghumphir / n. wandering

ghumti / n. turn

ghumto / n. veil

ghurki / n. bullying; unjustified demand

ghurnu / v. snore

ghus / n. bribe

ghusyaahaa / n. corrupt; bribetaker

ghyaampo / n. big earthen jar

gobar / n. cow dung

godaa / n. feet

gol / adj. round

golabaari / n. bombardment

goli haannu / v. shoot

gompa / n. tibetan buddhist monastery

gopaniyata / n. confidentiality

gopya / adj. confidential

goraa / adj. n. white; white man

goreto / n. trail

goro / adj. white

goraa / n. white man

gosthi / n. seminar

goth / n. cowshed

gothaalo / n. shepherd

graha / n. planet

grahan / n. eclipse

grishma / n. summer

guhu / n. human excrement

gulaabjaamun / n. a kind of sweet dish

gulaaph / n. rose

guliyo / adj. sweet

gumaaunu / v. lose

gun / n. merit; quality

gundaa / n. adj. hooligan; rascal

gundaagardi / n. hooliganism

gupta / adj. secret; hidden

guru / n. teacher

gurung / n. tribe living in central Nepal

gurudwaaraa / n. sikh temple

gyaan / n. knowledge

haad / n. bone

haai / n. yawn

haai garnu / v. yawn

haajir / a. present
haajiri / n. presence
haal / n. situation
haalat / n. state of affairs
haalai / for the time being
haalnu / v. put
haami /pron. we
haamro / adj. our
haangaa / n. branch
haani / n. damage
haank / n. challenge
haanknu / v. challenge, drive
haannu / v. hit; strike
haanthaap / competition
haar / n. neckless; defeat
haarnu / v. be defeated
haardik / adj. hearty
haasnu / v. laugh
haaso / n. laugh
haasyaaspad / adj. ridiculous
haataa / n. surroundings

haatti / n. elephant

haawaa / n. air

haawaapaani / n. climate

hagnu / v. shit

haijaa / n. cholera

hajaar / num. thousand

hajam / n. digestion

hajur / pron. you (honorific)

hairaan / adv. worried; exhausted

hak / n. right

hal / n. solution

halchal / n. movement

hal garnu / v. solve

halkaara / n. postman

hallaa / n. rumour

hallanu / v. shake

haluwa / n. sweet dish made of flour

haluko / adj. light

hamalaa / n. attack

hamalaa garnu / v. attack

hapkaaunu / v. reprimand; warn

hapsi / n. adj. black; negro
haptaa / n. week
harek / pron. each
hariyo / adj. green
hartaal / n. strike
hastihaad / n. ivory
hataar / n. hurry
hataar garnu / v. hurry
hataas hunu / v. be disappointed
hatiyaar / n. weapon
hatkadi / n. handcuff
hatpat / n. haste
hatyaa / n. killing; assassination
hatyaara / n. killer
hattaakatta / adj. strong
haushalaa / adj. n. courage
hawaaijahaaj / n. aeroplane
helaan / look down upon
hekkaa / n. memory
hepnu / v. look down upon
hernu / v. look

hidnu / v. walk

hijo / adv. yesterdays

hijoaaja / now a days

hilo / n. mud

hinsaa / n. violence

himaalaya / n. mountains north of Nepal

hiphaajat / n. care

hira / n. diamond

hinaaminaa / n. embezzlement

hirkaaunu / v. hit

hisaab / n. account

hit / n. well being; welfare

hitaishi / a. well wisher

hiun / n. snow

hiund / n. winter

hocho / adj. low

hosh / n. consciousness

hoshiyaar / adj. careful

hukkaa / n. hookah

hukum / n. command

hul / n. crowd

hulaak / n. postal service

hulmul / n. crowd

hulnu / v. get inside; penetrate

hundari / n. adj. rioter

hundi / n. money transaction

hunu / v. be

huri / n. storm

huttyaaunu / v. be swept away

ibi / n. enemity

ichchhaa / n. wish

ijaajat / n.permission

ijaajat patra / n. permit; authorization

ijjat / n. honour

ikh / n. jealousy

ilaakaa / n. area; region

ilam / n. knowledge; useful occupation; vocation

ilaam / n. district in eastern Nepal

ilami / adj. hard working; industrious

imaan / n. honest

imaandaar / n. adj. honest

inaam / n. prize

inaar / n. well

indra / n. deity in Hindu mythology

indrajaatraa / n. festival in Nepal falling in September

insaaph / n. justice

int / n. brick

irshyaa / n. jealousy

isaai / n. adj. christian

istri / n. iron

istri garnu / v. iron

iswar / n. god

jaado / adj. n. cold

jaado hunu / v. feel cold

jaagaran / n. awakening

jaagir / n. government service

jaagir khaanu / v. be in service

jaagnu / v. wake up

jagraam basnu / v. wake up all night in a religious
festival

jaanawar / n. animal

jaangar / n. alertness ; lack of idleness

jaangarilo / adj. n. alert; industrious

jaankaari / n. information

jaannu / v. know

jaanr/ n. rice beer

jaari / n. adultery

jaat / n.. caste

jaatiyata / n.. casteism

jaatraa / n. festival

jahaa / adv. where

jabarjasti / n.. violence; force

jadaau / adj. ornament having
jewels and precious stones

jadibuti / n. herbal medicine

jagaaunu / v. wake someone up

jagat / n. world

jagedaa / adj. n. standby

jaggaa / n. land

jahaaj / n. ship

jahaan / n. family; wife

jahile / adv. when

jain / n. religious group in India

jaj / n. judge

jajmaan / n. client of a priest

jal / n. water

jalaaunu / v. burn; set on fire

jalbidyut / n. hydroelectricity

jalpaan / n. tea party

jalshrot / n. water resources

jamghat / n. gathering

jamin / n. land

jamindaar / n. landlord

jamkaabhet / n. meeting by chance

jammaa / adj. n. total

jammaa garnu / v. gather

jamnu / v. freeze

janai / n. sacred thread

janajaati / n. tribal people

janaandolan / n. people's movement

janakpur / n. city in southern Nepal

janamat / n. referendum

janani / n. mother

jangal / n. jungle

jangali / adj; n. uncivilized

jangi / adj. relating to army
janjir / n. iron chain
janma / n. birth
janma bhumi / n. birthplace
janmajaat / adj. by birth
jandhan / n. men and material
jan ganana / n. population census
jan samhaar / n. genocide
jan samkhyaa / n. population
janata / n. people
janti / n. marriage procession
jap garnu / v. meditate with bead
jaraa / n. root
jaraayo / n. antelope
jarurat / n. necessity
jaruri / n. urgent
jas / n. appreciation
jastaa / n. zinc
jataasukai / adv. wherever
jatan / n. care
jathabhabi / adj. haphazard

jatil / adj. difficult

jau / n. barley

jawaab / n. reply

jawaan / adj. young

jawaani / n. youth

jaya / n. victory

jeb / n. pocket

jeb kaatnu / v. pick pocket

jehandaar / adj. intelligent

jethaa / n. property

jethaan / n. brother-in-law

jetho / adj. n. elder (first born)

jetho baatho / adj. responsible elder born

jhalak / n. glimpse

jhalkanu / v. shine

jhamjham / n. continuous rain

jhamtanu / v. jump to take by force

jhan / adj. more

jhandaa / n. flag

jhandai / adv. almost

jhaankri / n. witch doctor

jhaapat / n. slap

jhaar / n. grass

jhaarphuk / n. traditional medicine

jhaarnu / v. descent; get some money

jhadkelo chhoro / step son

jhagadaa / n. dispute

jhagadaa garnu / v. dispute; quarrel

jhagadiyaa / n. one of parties to dispute

jhatta / adv. at once

jhiknu / v. withdraw

jhingaa / n. fly

jhingati / n. roof made of bricky material

jhismise / n. dawn

jhok / n. anger

jhol / n. soup

jholi / n. bag

jhoraa / n. illegal settlements in forest land in the terai region of Nepal

jhukaaw / n. leaning

jhuknu / v. bend down; lean

jhusilkiraa / n. caterpillar

jhulaaunu / v. put off
jhundinu / v. hang
jhupro / n. cottage
jhuto / n. adj. false
jhyaal / n. window
jhyaaure / n. Nepalese folk song
jib / n. living being
jibikaa / n. livelihood
jib shaastra / n. biology
jibro / n. tongue
jiddi / n. obstinacy
jillaa / n. district
jilphi / n. sweet dish
jimmaa / n. charge; responsibility
jimmebaar / n. adj. responsible
jiraa / n. cummin seed
jirnoddhaar / n. renovation
jiskinu / v. tease; joke
jit / n. victory}
jitnu / v. win
jiu / n. body

jiundo / adv. alive

jiuni / property given by relatives for subsistence of elderly parents

jiwan / n. life

jiwani / n. biography

jiwikoparjan / n. livelihood

jo / pron. whoever

joban / n. youth

jodnu / v. join

jogaaunu / v. preserve

jogi / n. holy man

joipoi / n. wife-husband

jor / n. force; even number

josh / n. enthusiasm

jot / n. farming

jotnu / v. farm; cultivate

judhnu / v. fight

jukaa / n. leach; worm in intestine

julus / n. procession

jumso / adj. n. slow

jumraa / n. lice

jun / n. moonlight

jungaa / n. moustache

junkiri / n. firefly

jutaaunu / v. supply

jutho / n. food polluted by others; ritual impurity caused by death in the family

juttaa / n. shoe

juwaa / n. gambling

juwaadi / n. gambler

juwaa khelnu / v. gamble

jyaadaa / adv. more

jyaalaa / n. remuneration; wages

jyaami / daily hired labourer

jyaan / n. life

jyaanmaara / n. murderer

jyaamir / n. a kind of fruit

jyaapu / n. Newar farmer in Kathmandu valley

jyoti / n. light

jyotishi / n. adj. astrologer

kaabu / n. control

kaabu ma raakhnu / v. subdue

kaag / n. crow
kaagat / n. paper
kaagati / n. lemon
kaaj / n. work; deputation
kaakaa / n. uncle
kaakh / n. lap
kaal / n. time; death
kaali / n. hindu goddess
kaaligad / n. carpenter
kaalo / adj. black
kaalpanik / adj. imaginary
kaam / n. work
kaamadhenu / n. legendary cow in hindu scriptures
kaam garnu / v. work
kaami / n. smith
kaamkaaj / n. work
kaamnu / v. shiver
kaan / n. ear
kaano / adj. one eyed
kaanch / n. glass
kanchho / n. youngest born

kanchhi / n. youngest borri girl

kaandh / n. shoulder

kaangiyo / n. comb

kaankro / n. cucumber

kaanda / n. thorn

kaanun / n. law

kaaraagar / n. jail

kaaran / n. reason

kaarkhaana / n. factory

kaarobaar / n. business transaction

karindaa / n. clerk

kaarya / n. work

kaaryadal / n. task force

kaaryakaal / n. term

kaaryakaarini / n. board of directors

kaaryakartaa / n. worker

kaathar / adj. coward

kaatmaar / n. slaughter

kaatro / n. shround

kaayal / n. submitting

kaayam / adv. maintained; established

kabi / n. poet

kabitaa / n. poem

kabjaa / n. possession

kachchaa / adj. crude

kachhuwaa / n. tortoise

kadaa / adj. n. hard; tough

kadam / n. step

kadar / n. appreciation

kahaani / n. story

kahin / n. somewhere

kaidi / n. prisoner

kaile kaahin / adv. occasionally

kainchee / n. scissor

kaiphiyat / n. remarks

kaiyaun / adj. n. several

kal / n. machine

kalaa / n. art

kalaha / n. dispute

kalaakaar / n. artist

kalanki / adj. someone bringing disrepute

kalejo / n. liver

kalilo / adj. immature; young

kalpanaa / n. imagination

kalyaan / n. welfare

kamaai / n. earning

kamal / n. lotus

kamalo / adj. soft; delicate

kamaaro / n. slave

kamaaunu / v. earn

kami / n. shortage

kamij / n. shirt

kamilaa / n. ant

kamjor / adj. weak

kamjori / n. weakness

kammar / n. waist

kamse kam / at least

kangaal / n. bankrupt

kanikaa / n. rice grain pieces

kanjoos / n. miser

kantoor / n. box

kapadaa / v. clothing

kanyaaunu / v. scratch

kapaas / n. cotton
kapat / n. ill will
kapati / n. miser; treacherous
kapur / n. camphor
kar / n. tax
kardaataa / n. taxpayer
karang / n. rib
karaunti / n. saw
karib / prep. near
karjaa / n. loan
karma / n. destiny
karmachaari / n. official
karmi / n. carpenter
karunaa / n. piety
karuwaa / n. metal water pot
kaaryakaarini / executive
karyakram / n. programme
karyaalaya / n. office
kasaai / n. butcher
kasari / adv. how
kastha / n. wood

kasnu / v. tighten

kasrat / n. exercise

kasur / n. guilt

kasto / adv. how

kasturi / n. musk

kata / adv. where

katai / adv. somewhere

kathor / adj. cruel; harsh

kati / adv. how much ?

katro / adv. how big?

kausi / n. rooftop terrace

ke / adj. what ?

kehi / adj. some

kernu / v. cross question

kelaaunu / v. cull

kendra / n. centre

kendriya / adv. central

keraa / n. banana

kesh / n. hair

keshar / n. saffron

ketaaketi / n. children

keti / n. girl

keto / n. boy

kewal / adv. only

khabar / n. news

khadga / n. sword

khadya / n. food

khairo / adj. grey

khajaanaa / n. treasury

khanjaanchi / n. treasurer

khajur / n. date

khalak / n. family

khalbal / n. noise

khallo / adj. tasteless

khalti / n. pocket

khaadal / n. ditch

khaali / adj. empty

khaancho / n. need

khaadnu / v. pack

khaandaan / n. family

khaani / n. mine

khaanaa / n. food

khaanu / v. eat

khaas / adj. special

khaat / n. wooden cot

khandan / n. rebuttal

khannu / v. dig

khanyaaunu / v. pour

khar / n. thatch; grass

kharaab / adj. bad

kharaani / n. ash

kharaayo / n. rabbit

kharcha / n. expenses; expenditure

khardaar / n. adj. low level government clerk

kharid / n. purchase

khasi / n. castrated goat

khasnu / v. fall down

khasro / adj. rough

khatam / n. finished

khataaunu / v. depute; send

khatara / n. danger

khauranu / v. shave

khed / n. regret

khednu / v. chase; pursue

khel / n. game; play

khelaadi / n. sportsman; player

khelnu / v. play

khet / n. farm

khetaalaa / n. farmer

khetipaati / n. farming

khinna / adj. n. sad

khisi / n. mockery

khiyaa / n. rust

khochyaaunu / v. limp

khoj / n. search

khoji / n. search

khoki / n. cold

kholaa / n. stream

kholnu / v. open

khol / n. cover

khopaaunu / v. vaccinate

khor / n. jail

khosnu / v. dismiss

khub / adv. very

khudraa / n. small change in coins

khulaa / adj. open

khulnu / v. open

khumchinu / v. shrink

khurkinu / v. scrape

khursaani / n. chilly

khushi / n. happiness

khutta / n. feet

ki / conj. or

killaa / n. fortress

kina / adv. why

kinaki / conj. because

kinaara / n. bank

kinnu / v. buy

kipat / n. system of landownership in eastern hills

kiphaayat / n. thrift

kiraa / n. bug

kiran / n. ray

kiraaya / n. rent

kirte / n. forgery

kishor / n. adolescent

kirti / n. fame

kisaan / n. farmer

kismis / n. raisin

kitaab / n. book

kitaanu / n. germs

ko / pron. who?

kodaalo / n. mattock with handle

kodo / n. rye

kohi / n. somebody

koilaa / n. coal

koili / n. cuckoo

kolaahal / n. uproar

kopilaa / n. bud

kornu / v. scratch

koshelee / n. present; gift

kosi / n. one of major rivers of Nepal

koshish / n. attempt

kot / n. coat; jacket

kothi / n. mole

kottyaaunu / v. broach

krishi / n. agriculture

kritagya / adj. n. grateful
kritrim / adj. artificial
kriyaa / n. ritual mourning
krodh / n. anger
krodhi / adj. angry
kuchchinu / v. crumpled; bent
kuhinu / v. rot; get spoiled
kuire / slang. white man
kukur / n. dog
kulachchhini / n. bringing bad omen
kulo / n. channel
kumaari / n. living goddess of Kathmandu
kun / pron. which
kunai maanis / n. somebody
kunai kisimle / adv. somehow
kunai kura / n. something
kunai belaa / n. sometime
kunai maatraamaa / adv. somewhat
kupro / adj. hunchback
kuraa / n. talk; thing
kurilo / n. asparagus

kurnu / v. watch; wait
kursi / n. chair
kusle / n. a caste of newars in the valley
kusta rog / n. leprosy
kut / adj. n. cunning
kutniti / n. diplomacy
kutnitigya / n. diplomat
kutkute / adj. ticklish
kutumba / n. relative
kuwaa / n. well
laabaaris / adv. unclaimed
laabh / n. profit; gain
laabhdaayak / adv. profitable
laabhamsha / n. dividend
laachaar / adj. helpless
laachhi / adj. coward
laadnu / v. load
laagat / n. cost
laagi / prep. for
laagu / adv. intoxicating
laagu garnu / v. enforce

laahaa / n. sealing wax

laai / prep. for; to

laaj / n. shame

laakh / numb. one hundred thousand

laalach / adj. greed

laal / adj. red

laaligurans / n. rhododendron

laalmohar / n. royal seal

laalten / n. lantern

laamaa / n. tibetan monk

laamkhuttee / n. mosquito

laamo / adj. long

laanu / v. take along

laaparbaahi / n. negligence

laat / n. kick

latthi / n. stick

laato / adj. dumb

laaunu / v. wear

laayak / adj. n. fit; worthy

ladaai / n. war

laddu / n. sweet dish

ladnu / v. fight
lagan / n. dedication
lagaani / n. investment
lagaarnu / v. chase
lagaayat / adv. including
lagaaunu / v. wear
lahar / n. wave
laharaa / n. ivy
lakhetnu / v. pursue
lakhpati / n. rich man; one who owns one hundred
thousand rupees
lakshmi / n. goddess of wealth
lakshya / n. aim
lalitkala / n. fine arts
lambaai / n. length
lami / n. broker for marriage
langado / adj. n. lame
lasun / n. garlic
lassi / n. sweet drink made or curd
lat / n. habit
lataa / n. ivy

latthi / n. stick

laththinu / v. come under spell; hypnotized

lauro / n. support; stick

le / prep. by; with

lek / n. highlands

lekh / n. article; writing

lekhak / n. writer

lekhaapadhi / n. correspondence

lekhnu / v. write

letnu / v. lie down

lilaam / n. auction

limbu / n. tribe living in eastern hills

lichchi / n. a kind of fruit

linga / n. male sexual organ; gender

linu / v. take

lipi / n. script

lipnu / v. smear

lobh / n. greed

lobhi / adj. greedy

logne / n. husband

logne maanchhe / n. male

lok / adj. public

lok sewaa aayog / n. public service commission

lop hunu / v. disappear

lokaachaar / n. social behaviour

luchcho / adj. cunning

lugaa / n. clothes

lukaaunu / v. hide

lulo / adj. loose; limp

lumbini / n. birthplace of Buddha in southern Nepal

lure / adj. n. weak; feeble

lut / n. loot

luto / n. scabies

lwaang / n. cloves

lyaapche / n. thumbprint

maa / prep. at; in; on

maachha / n. fish

maadal / n. drum

maadhyam / adj. medium

maadhyamik / adj. n. secondary

maagh / n. month in Nepalese calendar

maagne / n. beggar

maahilo / n. adj. second eldest

maaiju / n. aunt (maternal uncle's wife)

maaiti / n. women's parents home

maajh / n. centre

maajhi / n. fisherman

maajhnu / v. clean

maakho / n. fly

maakuraa / n. spider

maal / n. baggage; property

maalaa / n. garland

maali / n. gardener

maalik / n. owner; master

maamaa / n. maternal uncle

maamuli / adj. ordinary; simple

maanab / n. mankind

maanab adhikaar / n. human rights

maanasik / adj. mental

manik / n. ruby

maanis / n. man

maannu / v. obey; agree

maansaahaari / n. adj. non-vegetarian

maanya / adj. respected
maanyataa / n. value; belief
maapaako / adj. tough; wicked
maaphi / n. forgiveness
maaphi garnu / v. forgive
maarg / n. way; road
maarnu / v. kill
maar kaat / n. disturbance; killing
maas / n. month
maasik / adj. n. monthly
maasnu / v. destroy; spend
maataa / v. mother
maateko / adv. spiled; drunk
maathi / prep . above; up; over; on
maato / n. soil; earth
maatra / adv. prep. only
maatri bhaasaa / n. mother tongue
maauri / n. honey bee
maawali / n. maternal uncle's house
maayaa / n. love
ma / pron. I

machaan / n. platform in national parks for viewing wildlife

madhes / n. southern part of Nepal also called the terai

madhesia / n. inhabitant of the terai belonging to Indian origin

madhur / adj. sweet

madhya / n. center

madhyam / adj. central; middle madira / n. liquor

magaj / n. brain

magar / n. tribe living in western hills

mahaa / adj. big

mahaadesh / n. continent

mahaajan / n. merchant

mahaakaali / n. river forming western boundary of Nepal

mahaalekha parikshyak / n. auditor general

mahaamaari / n. epidemic

mahaarog / n. leprosy

mahaayuddha / n. great war

mahaan / adj. n. great

mahal / n. building; palace

mahango / adj. expensive

mahaaraja / n. ruler of a princely state

mahaaraajadhiraaj / n. king of Nepal

mahaaraani / n. queen

mahaasaagar / n. ocean

mahaatma / n. adj. great soul; title given to Gandhi

mahatwa / n. importance

mahatwapurna / adj. n. important

mahendra / n. king of Nepal from 1955 to 1972

mahi / n. butter milk

mahimaa / n. greatness

mahinaa / n. month

mahinaawaari / n. wage

maidaa / n. flour

maidaan / n. plain

mailo / adj. n. dirty

main / n. wax

maintol / n. lantern

maitri / n. friendship

maiyaan / n. girl

majboot / n. adj. strong
majdoor / n. worker
majdoori / n. labour; remuneration
makal / n. fire stove
makhan / n. butter
makhmal / n. velvet
makkinu / v. decay
malaami / n. funeral procession
malam / n. ointment
malilo / adj. n. fertile
malnu / v. rub
mamataa / n. affection
man / n. mind
man laagnu / v. feel like doing
man parnu / v. like
manaahi / adv. prohibited
mandap / n. pavilion
mandir / n. temple
mangal / adj. auspicious
mangalbaar /n. tuesday
mani / n. jewel

manjan / n. toothpaste
manjur / adv. agreed
manobritti / n. tendency
manobigyaan / n. science of human mind
manoranjan / n. entertainment
manpardo / adj. at will
manpari / adv. arbitrarily
mansaaya / n. intention
mantra / n. sacred verses for chanting
mantri / n. minister
mantri-mandal / n. cabinet
marammat / n. repair
mard / adj. n. male
markanu / v. twist
marnu / v. die
marubhumi / n. desert
maryaadaa / n. respect; decorum
masaalaa / n. spices
masaan / n. cremation grounds
mashaal / n. name of leftist political party; flame
masi / n. ink

masino / adj. fine
masjid / n. mosque
masyaudaa / n. adj. draft
masyauraa / n. dried vegetable
mat / n. opinion
matahat / prep. under
matar / n. peas
matalab / n. interest; meaning
matalabi / n. selfish
mattitel / n. kerosene oil
matwaali / adj. n. castes which drink alcohol meaning
those other than brahmins and some chhetris
maukaa / n. chance
maulik / n. adj. original
maun / n. silence; silent
mausam / n. weather
mayur / n. peacock
mech / n. chair
mehanat / n. hard work
megh / n. cloud
melmilaap / n. reconciliation

melaa / n. fair; exhibition
mero / poss . pron. mine
merudanda / n. spinal cord
metnu / v. erase
mewaa / n. papaya
michnu / v. encroach; transgress
mijas / n. manner; nature
milaap / n. getting together; reconciliation
milaapatra / n. document ratifying reconciliation
between two disputed parties in a court case
milaaunu / v. bring together; adjust
milaawat / n. adulteration
mildo / adj. suitable
milnu / v. agree; meet
mim / n. white woman
misaaunu / v. mix
mit / n. friend whose friendship is formalized by ritual
friendship
mitra / n. friend
mlechha / adj. non-believer; non Hindu
moh / n. illusion

mohini / n. spell
mohar / n. fifty paisa coin
mohi / n. tenant farmer
mojaa / n. sock
moksha / n. salvation
mol / n. price
molbhaau / n. bargain
molbhaau garnu / v. bargain
mosambi / n. orange
moso / n. black soot
moti / n. pearl
moto / adj. fat
muchhnu / v. involve
muddaa / n. court case
mudraa / n. currency
mudraa-sphiti / n. inflation
mudnu / v. shave the head
mudho / n. log
mudrak / n. printer
mugga / n. coral
muhaar / n. face

mukh / n. face
mukhya / adj. main
mukhiyaa / n. chief
mukkaa / n. blow
mukta / adj. free
mukti / n. emancipation
mukut / n. crown
mul / n. adj. main; source
mulaa / n. radish
multabi / adv. suspended
mulyaa / n. price
mumaa / n. mother
muni / n. hermit
muntaa / n. baby soother
muntira / adv. below
murali / n. flute
murdaa / n. dead body
murkha / adj. n. fool
musalmaan / n. adj. Moslem
musaldhaar / adj. torrential
mushkil / adj. difficult

muskaan / n. smile

muskuraaunu / v. smile

musaa / n. mouse

mut / n. urine

mutnu / v. urinate

mutaabik / adv. according

muththi / n. fist

mutu / n. heart

mwaai / n. kiss

na / negative when added before a verb

naach / n. dance

naachghar / n. theatre

naachnu / v. dance

naadaan / adj. n. innocent

naag / n. serpent

naagarik / n. citizen

naagariktaa / n. citizenship

naaghnu / v. go beyond; cross over

naaike / n. chief; leader

naajaayaj / adj. illegal

naaito / n. navel

naak / n. nose
naal / n. umbical cord
naalaa / n. stream
naalish / n. civil suit
naam / n. name
naami / adj. famous
naan / n. bread usually made in western India
naango / adj. naked
naap / n. measurement
naaphaa / n. profit
naapnu / v. measure
naaraa / n. slogan
naari / n. woman
naash / n. destruction
naasnu / v. destroy; spoil
naaspaati / n. pear
naastik / n. adj. atheist
naataa / n. relationship
naatak / n. drama
naati / n. grandson
naatini / n. grand-daughter

naba / adj. new
naba barsha / n. new year
nadi / n. river
nagada / n. drum
nagad / n. cash
nagar / n. city
nagarpaalikaa / n. municipality
nagich / adv. near
nahar / n. canal
najar / n. look
najaraana / n. present; gift
nakacharo / adj. n. shameless
nakal / n. copying
nakkali / adj. not genuine
naksaa / n. map
nakshyatra / n. planet
nal / n. tap
number / n. number
namaste / n. salutation; good bye; good morning
namra / adj. polite
namrataa / n. politeness

namunaa / n. sample

nang / n. nail

nar / n. man

narak / n. hell

naram / adj. soft

naramaailo / adj. unpleasant

naraamro / adj. bad

nariwal / n. coconut

nashaa / n. nerve; intoxication

natijaa / n. result

natra / adv. otherwise

naulo / adj. new

nauni / n. butter

nayaa / adj. new

nel / n. handcuff

netaa /n. leader

netritwa / n. leadership

newaar / n. inhabitants of Kathmandu valley who made many works of art

nibaas / n. dwelling

nibaasi / n. inhabitant

nibedan / n. application; request

nibhaaunu / v. extinguish

nibuwaa / n. lemon

nich / adj. mean

nichornu / v. squeeze

nidaaunu / v. sleep

nidar / adj. unafraid

nidaar / n. forehead

nidra laagnu / v. feel sleepy

nihun / n. pretext

nihuranu / v. bend down; humble

niji / adj. personal

nijaamati / civil

nijaamati sewa / civil service

nikai / adj. many

nikat / n. adj. near

nikaalnu / v. take out

nikhannu / v. repossess mortgaged property

niklanu / v. emerge; come out

niko hunu / v. cure

nikunj / n. park

nilnu / v. swallow
nilo / adj. blue
nimto / n. invitation
nindaa / n. abuse
nindaa garnu / v. abuse
niparsi / adj. day after tomorrow
nipun / n. expert
niraamish / adj. non-vegetarian
nirantar / adj. continuously
nirarthak / n. nonsense
niraashaa / n. disappointment
nirbibaad / adj. non-controversial
nirbikalpa / n. without alternative
nirbirodh / n. without opposition
nirdayi / adj. cruel
nirdosh / adj. innocent
nirikshyan / n. inspection
nirmal / adj. clear
nirnaya / n. decision
nirog / adj. healthy
nisahaya / adj. helpless

nisaaph / n. justice
nishaanaa / n. target
nisiddha / adj. banned
niskanu / v. emerge
nissandheh / n. without doubt
nithur / n. cruel
niti / n. policy
nitishaastra / n. diplomacy
niwaaran / n. alleviation; removal
niyam / n. rule; regulation
niyamit / adj. regular
niyantran / n. control
niyukta / adj. appointed
nokar / n. servant
nokari / n. service
nuhaaunu / v. take bath
nuhunu / v. bow down; be submissive
nun / n. salt
nunilo / adj. salty
nwaaran / n. ceremony ten days after birth
nyaano / adj. warm

nyaauri / n. mongoose
nyaaya / n. justice
nyayaadhish / n. judge
ochchhyaan / n. bedding
odaar / n. cave
ogatnu / v. occupy
ohar dohar garnu / v. walk to and fro
okhar / n. walnut
okhati / n. medicine
oraalo / n. descent
oraalnu / v. bring down
orlanu / v. descend go down
osaarnu / v. transport
ossinu / v. dampen
oth / n. lip
paachak / adj. digestive in ayurvedic medicine
paagal / adj. mad; insane
paahunaa / n. guest
paailo / n. step
paakhandi / adj. n. hypocrite
paakhe / n. adj. uncultured

paakhi / n. blanket made in Nepal

paaknu / v. ripen;

paako / adj. mature

paal / n. tent

paali / n. turn

paalungo / n. spinach

paan / n. beetle leaf

paanaa / n. page

paanch / num. five

paangro / n. wheel

paani / n. water

paap / n. sin

paapi / n. sinner

paar / prep. across (on the other side)

paarbati / shiva's consort

paasne / n. ceremony in which a six month old child
is given his first rice serving

paat / n. leaf

paataki / n. sinner

paath / n. lesson

paathak / n. reader

paatho / n. buffalo's offspring
paati / n. roadside inn
paatro / n. calendar
paau / n. foot
paaunu / v. receive
paauroti / n. bread
paban / n. wind
pabitra / adj. pure; holy
pachhaadi / adv. behind
pachhi laagnu / v. follow
pachhuto / n. repentance
padhnu / v. study; read
paglanu / v. melt
pahaad / n. hills
pahaadi / n. hillfolks
pahalmaan / adj. n. athlete; wrestler
pahilo / adj. first
pahiro / n. landslide
paidal / on foot
paincho / n. loan
paisa / n. money

pakaaunu / v. cook
pakhaalnu / v. wash
pakkaa / adj. certain; permanent
pakranu / v. catch; arrest
palang / n. bed
paltanu / v. turn over
panaati / n. great grandson
panchaayat / n. council of five; system of government
in Nepal from 1962 to 1990
panchhyaaunu / v. get rid of
panchhi / n. bird
panero / n. water collection point
pani / adv. also
paraal / n. straw
parakram / n. bravery
parbat / n. mountains
parbate / n. one who lives in the mountains
parchaa / n. leaflet
pardaa / n. veil; curtain
parewaa / n. pigeon
paribaar / n. family

paribaar niyojan / n. family planning

paribartan / n. change

parichaya / n. introduction; acquaintance

parikshaa / n. examination

parinaam / n. result

parishram / n. hard labour

parishrami / n. adj. laborious; industrious

parkhaal / n. outer wall

parkhanu / v. wait

parnu / v. get involved

paropakaar / n. philanthropy

parsi / adv. day after tomorrow

pasal / n. shop

paschim / n. west

pashu / n. animal

pashupatinaath / n. most famous temple of Nepal

path / n. road

pati / n. husband

patibrata / adj. n. devoted to husband

patni / n. wife

patra / n. letter

patukaa / n. belt

patyaar / n. trust

patyaaunu / v. trust

paudanu / v. swim

paushtik aahaar / n. nutritious food

peshagi / n. advance of money

pet / n. stomach

pewaa / n. private property given by husband to wife

phaandnu / v. destroy trees in forest

phaalnu / v. throw away

phaatnu / v. split

phajul / adj. nonsense

phakir / n. moslem holy man

phal / n. fruit

phalahaar / n. diet of food consisting of fruit

phalaam / n. iron

phalaano / pron. somebody

phandaa / n. net

pharaakilo / adj. wide

phariyaa / n. sari

pharkanu / v. return

pharkaaunu / v. send back
phasaad / adj. difficult
phasnu / v. get involved
phataahi / n. lie
phataahaa / adj. n. liar
phatphat / n. useless talk
phauj / n. army
phaujdaari / adj. criminal
phauji / adj. armed
pheri / adv. again
pheharisht / n. list
phikri / n. anxiety
phiraadpatra / n. suit filed by plaintiff in court of law
phirtaa / n. return
phitta / n. lace
phohar / adj. dirty
phohari / n. dirty
phokaa / n. bubble
phokat / adj. in vain
phuknu / v. blow; expand; treat
phul / n. egg; flower

phulnu / v. flower
phulbaari / n. garden
phuphu / n. aunt (father's sister)
phursat / n. spare time
phurunga parnu / v. be happy
phusro / adj. grey
phut / n. split
phutaaunu / v. cause a split
phutnu / v. split
pinaas / n. sinus
pinjara / n. cage
pip / n. pus
pir / n. worry
piro / n. spicy; hot
pisaab / n. urine
pittal / n. brass
pitnu / v. hit
piunu / v. drink alcohol
pohar / adv. preceeding year
pokhari / n. pond
pokhnu / v. spill

poshan / n. nourishment

posnu / v. nourish

pote / n. beads used in a neckless

praachin / adj. ancient

praakritik / adj. natural

praan / n. life

praarthanaa / n. prayer

prachaar / n. propoganda

pradesh / n. province; state

pradarshini / n. exhibition

pradhaan / adj. chief

pradhaan mantri / n. prime minister

prajaa / n. subject; people

prajaatantra / n. democracy

prakaash / n. light

prakaashak / n. publisher

prakriti / n. nature

pramaan / n. proof

pranaayaam / n. breathing exercise

prasaad / n. blessing or favour from deity

prasamsaa / n. praise

prasasta / adj. adequate
prashna / n. question
prasthaan / n. departure
prataapi / n. adj. powerful
prathaa / n. custom
pratigyaa / n. promise
pratibandha / n. restriction
pratyaksha / n. evident
prayatna / n. attempt
prem / n. love
prem garnu / v. love
premi / lover (m)
premikaa / lover (f)
prerana / n. inspiration
priti / n. affection
puchchhar / n. tail
puchhnu / v. wipe out
pugdo / adj. sufficient
pugnu / v. reach; be adequate
pujaa / n. worship
pujaa garnu / v. worship

pujaari / n. person taking care of a temple
pul / n. bridge
punji / n. capital
punjibaad / n. capitalism
puraa / adj. full
puraano / adj. old
purba / n. east
purohit / n. priest
puryaaunu / v. send off
pustak / n. book
pustakaalaya / n. library
putali / n. butterfly
pwaal / n. hole
pyaaj / n. onion
pyaalaa / n. cup
pyaaso / adj. thirsty
raahadaani / n. passport
raaj / n. rule
raaja / n. king
raajbandi / n. political prisoner
raaj darbaar / n. royal palace

raaj dhaani / n. capital
raaj doot / n. ambassador
raaj gaddi / n. throne
raaj guru / n. royal preceptor
raaji / adj. willing
raajkumaar / n. prince
raajkumaari / n. princess
raajmaa / n. kidney beans
raajniti / n. politics
raajanitigya / n. politician
raajtantra / n. monarchy
raajyaabhishek / n. coronation
raakhnu / v. put
raakshyas / n. demon
raam / n. hindu deity
raamrari / adv. well
raamro / adj. good; beautiful
raana / n. oligarchy which ruled Nepal for a century
raango / n. male buffalo
raani / n. queen
raasaayanik / adj. chemical

raashtra / n. country
raashtriya / adj. national
raashtriyata / n. nationalism
raat / n. night
raato / adj. red
raaya / n. advice; opinion
raayo / n. mustard leaf
ra / conj. and
rachana / n. literary work
raddi / adj. n. useless
ragat / n. blood
rahanu / v. remain
rahar / n. interest; a kind of lentil
raharlaagdo / adj. interesting
rahasya / n. mystery
rajaai / n. quilt
rajaswalaa / adj. woman having period
rajat jayanti / n. silver jubilee
raksi / n. liquor
rakshya / n. protection
ramaailo / adj. pleasant

ramaaunu / v. like; be pleased
ramita / n. interesting spectacle
randi / n. prostitute
rang / n. adj. color
rangeen / adj. colourful
ras / n. juice
rasaayan shastra / n. chemistry
rasbari / n. sweet dish
rasid / n. receipt
rasik / adj. interesting and outgoing person
rath / n. chariot
ratnu / v. be tamed
raun / n. hair
rekhaankan / n. alignment
rel / n. train
resham / n. silk
rijhaaunu / v. please
riksaa / n. vehicle pulled by a bicycle
rin / n. debt
rini / n. debtor
rikaapi / n. plate

ris / n. anger

risaaera / adv. angrily

risaaeko / adj. angry

riti thiti / n. custom

ritto / n. season

ritu / n. season

rochak / adj. likable

rodighar / n. disco like club among gurungs in hills of west Nepal

rog / n. disease

rogi / n. patient

rojgaar / n. employment

rojnu / v. select

roknu / v. stop

roktok / n. stoppage

ropaai / n. cultivation

ropnu / v. cultivate

roti / n. bread

ruchaaunu / v. prefer; like

rughaa / n. cold

rujhnu / v. get wet in rain

rukh / n. tree
rukho / adj. rough; uninteresting
rumaal / n. handkerchief
runche / adj. weeping
runu / v. weep
rup / n. beauty
rupmati / adj. beautiful
rupiyaa / n. rupees
rudhi / n. superstition
ruju garnu / v. check
ryaal / n. saliva
saabik / n. post
saabun / n. soap
saachhi / n. witness
saada / n. adj. simple
saadhan / n. means; resources
saadhana / n. exercise
saande / n. ox
saadhe / adj. half past (hour)
saadhu / n. holy man
saadhu bhaai / n. brother in law (wife's sisters husband)

saag / n. spinach
saagar / n. sea
saahas / n. courage
saaheb / n. respected person
saahitya / n. literature
saahro / adj. hard
saahu / n. merchant
saahrai / adj. very
saaino / n. relationship
saait / n. auspicious occasion
saajhaa adj. n. common; co-operative
saajhedaar / n. partner
saajhedaari / adj. partnership
saakshaat / adj. incarnate in person
saakshi / n. witness
saakshi dinu / v. testify
saakshi bakaaunu / v. take evidence
saakshi baknu / v. give evidence
saal / n. a kind of tree found in Nepal
saala khaala / adj. average
saal basaal / adv. annually

saali / n. sister-in-law
saalo / n. brother-in-law
saal tamaam / n. year end
saamaajik / n. social
saamaan / n. things; goods
saamaanya / adj. ordinary
saamanta / n. feudal
saamanti / adj. feudal
saamarthya / n. ability
saamel / n. assemblage
saamu / in front of
saamraajya / n. empire
saamraajyabaad / n. imperialism
saamyabaad / n. communism
saamyabaadi / n. communist
saanchnu / v. store
saancho / n. truth
saanghu / n. culvert; small bridge
saanghuro / adj. narrow
saanglo / n. cockroach
saani / n. adj. small girl

saano / n. adj. small boy

saanobaa / n. uncle (mother's sister's husband)

saantwanaa / n. consolation

saapat / n. loan

saapat linu / v. borrow

saaph / adj. n. clean

saar / n. essence

saaraa / n. adj. entire; whole

saari / n. women dress in Nepal and India

saarki / n. cobbler

saasu / n. mother-in-law

saat / n. seven

saataa / n. week

saath / adv. together

saathi / n. friend; companion

saatnu / v. exchange

saato-putlo / n. consciousness

saaun / n. capital outlay

saaun / n. month in Nepali calendar

saawadhaan / n. adj. careful

sab / adj. all

sabaal / n. question
sab bhandaa dherai / adj. most
sabhaa / n. assembly; council
sabhaapati / n. chairman
sabhya / adj. civilized; cultured
sabhyataa / n. civilization
sabji / n. green vegetable
sachcharitra / n. having good character
sachet / adj. alert
sachib / n. secretary
sachibaalaya / n. secretariat
sachyaaunu / v. correct
sadaa/ adv. always
sadaachaari / adv. well behaved
sadak / n. road
sadar / n. capital city
sadasya / n. member
sadbhaabanaa / n. goodwill
sadhain / adv. always
saghaaunu / v. help
sagol / n. adj. joint family

saha-astitwa / n. co-existence
saha-kaari / adj. co-operative
sahansheel / adj. tolerant
sahanu / v. tolerate
sahaanubhuti / n. sympathy
sahar / b. city
sahaaraa / n. support
sahasikshya / n. co-education
sahaayak / n. adj. assistant
sahaayata / n. help; assistance
sahayog / n. co-operation
sahi / n. signature; correct
sahi garnu / v. sign
sajaaya / n. punishment
sajaaunu / v. decorate
sajaawat / n. decoration
sajilo / adj. easy
sajjan / n. gentleman
sakesamma / as much as possible
sakht / adj. n. extreme; hard
saknu / v. able to; can

salaha / n. locust
salaai / n. match
salaam / n. salutation
salkaaunu / v. set fire
sallaha / n. advice
sallahakaar / n. advisor
samaachaar / n. news
samaachaarpatra / n. newspaper
samaadhi / n. meditation; place of burial; cremation
samaaj / n. society
samaajbaad / n. socialism
samaajbaadi / n. communist
samaalnu / v. take care of
samaan / adj. equal
samaaroh / n. ceremony
samanbaya / n. co-ordination
samarpan / n. dedication
samartha / n. adj. capable
samasta / adj. n. entire
samasyaa / n. problem
samaatnu / v. catch hold of

samaya / n. time
sambaad / n. dialogue
sambaad-data / n. correspondent
sambaidhaanik / n. adj. constitutional
sambandh / n. relation; connection
sambandhi / n. relative
sambat / n. name of year in Nepali calendar
sambhaabana / n. possibility
sambhaabyata / n. feasibility
sambhab / adj. n. possible
sambidhaan / n. constitution
samdhi / n. son in law's father
samet / adv. together with
sameep / adv. near
samiti / n. society; committee; council
samjhanaa / n. memory
samjhaaunu / v. explain
samjhanu / v. remember
samjhautaa / n. understanding
samma / n. level; to
sammati / n. approval

sammelan / n. meeting
sampaadak / n. editor
sampaadakiya / adj. editorial
sampaadan / n. editing
sampanna / adj. n. affluent
samparka / n. contact
sampatti / n. wealth
sampradaya / n. community; religious group
sampradayabad / n. communalism
sampurna / adj. entire
samraat / n. emperor
samudra / n. ocean; sea
samuh / n. crowd
samyam / n. restraint
samyog / n. coincidence
samyukta / adv. united
samukta raajya / united states
samyukta raastra / united nations
sanaakhat garnu / v. testify
sanaatan / adj. old; continuing
sanak / n. whim

sanaki / n. whimsical
sanchaalak / n. director
sanchaalak samiti / board of directors
sanchaya / n. saving
sanchaar / n. communication
sanchaya kosh / n. provident fund
sancho / adj. n. in good health; well
sandarbha / n. context
sandesh / n. message
sandhi / n. treaty
sandhiaar / n. property owner of adjacent property
sandhyaa / n. evening
sanga / adv. together; with
sangam / n. confluence
sangamarmar / n. marble
sangat / n. company
sangeet / n. music
sangeetagya / n. musician
sangraha / n. collection
sanhaar / n. destruction
sankalpa / n. determination

sankat / n. crisis
sankhyaa / n. number
sankirna / adj. narrow
sankoch / n. hesitation
sankraanti / n. first day of Nepali month
sankshipta / adj. brief
sansad / n. parliament
sansaar / n. world
sansodhan / n. correction; revision
sanskaar / n. upbringing
sanskriti / n. culture
santa / n. saint
santosh / n. satisfaction
santushta / adv. satisfied
sapana / n. dream
saphaa / adj. clean
saphaai / n. cleanliness
saphal / adj. n. successful
saphalata / n. success
sapranu / v. improve
saptaah / n. week

saral / adj. simple

saraap / n. curse

saraswati / n. goddess of learning

sarbamaanya / adj. revered by all

sarbanaam / pronoun

sarbasaadhaaran / n. common man

sarbasya / n. entire assets; confiscation

sarbesarbaa / all in all

sarbochha / adj. supreme

sardar / adj. average

sardaar / n. leader; title given to all sikhs

sarkaar / n. government

sarkaari / adj. governmental

sarnu / v. move; shift

sarokaar / n. concern; interest

sarpa / n. snake

saruwaa / adj. contagious; transfer

sasto / adj. cheap

sasuralli / house of father-in-law

sasuro / n. father-in-law

satarka / adj. alert

satkaar / n. hospitality

sattal / n. roadside resting place; inn

satta patta / n. mutual exchange

satya / adj. true

saugaat / n. gift; tribute

sautaa / n. co-wife

sawaa / adj. one and quarter

seknu / v. roast; apply heat therapy

sekuwaa / adj. roasted

sel / n. dish made of flour

senaa / n. army

serophero / n. surroundings

seto / adj. white

sewa / n. service

sewak / n. servant

shaan / n. pride; shwowing off

shaanti / n. peace

shaanti kshetra / n. zone of peace

shaashak / n. ruler

shaastra / n. religious scripture

shaiyaa / n. bedding

shaayad / adv. perhaps
shabda / n. word
shakti / n. power
shanibaar / n. saturday
sharad / n. autumn
sharam / n. shame
sharan / n. asylum
sharanaarthi / n. refugee
shareer / n. body
shataabdi / n. century
shatru / adj. n. enemy
sheel / n. character
shesh / n. remainder
shikaar / n. hunting
shikaari / n. hunter
shikshya / n. education; teaching
shikshyak / n. teacher
shir / n. head
shirshak / n. heading; title
shishi / n. bottle
shishta / adj. cultured; well mannered

shistaachaar / n. courtesy
shital / adj. n. cool
sithil / adj. loose
shobha / n. beauty
shoshak / adj. exploiter
shoshan / n. exploitation
shraddhaa / n. devotion
sharaddha / n. annual mourning ceremony for parents
sharm / n. labour
shramik / n. labourer
shram-daan / n. voluntary labour contribution
shrestha / adj. n. superior; a caste among Newars
shree / used in front of names to indicate Mr.
shreemati / used in front of names to indicate Mrs.
shubha / adh. n. good; auspicious
shubhechchha / n. good wishes
shubhakaamanaa / greetings
shuddha / adj. pure
shuddhi / n. purification
shudra / n. member of lowest caste
shukra baar / n. friday

shunya / n. zero

shuru / n. beginning

shuru garnu / v. begin

siddhanta / n. theory

siddhaaunu / v. finish off

siddhinu / v. finish

sikarmi / adj. n. carpenter

sikarni / n. sweet dish made from yogurt

sikaaunu / v. instruct; teach

sikista / adj. seriously ill, serious

sikka / n. coin

siknu / v. learn

silsilaa / n. series; order

simaanaa / n. boundary

simi / n. french bean

sinchaai / n. irrigation

sindur / n. red powder on the forehead put by married women

singaar / n. decoration

singha / n. lion

singo / adj. whole

sipaahi / n. soldier

sipaalu / adj. n. expert

siphaarish / n. recommendation

siphaarish garnu / v. recommend

sirjana / n. creation

sisaakalam / n. pencil

sita / adv. together

sittal / n. cool

siyo / n. needle for sewing

smaarak / n. memorial

smriti / n. memory

sochaai / n. thinking

sochnu / v. think

sodhpoochh / n. enquiry

soharnu / n. gather up

sokh / n. spending to have good time

sojho / n. adj. simple; direct

sombaar / n. monday

somat / n. etiquette

sosnu / v. absorb

sristi / n. creation

sthaan / n. place; temple
sthaaniya / adj. local
stuti / n. praise
subba / n. name of a post in administrative service; name among the limbus
subidhaa / n. convenience
subistaa / n. comfort
suchanaa / n. information
suchi / n. list; urine
suchi-patra / n. catalogue
sudhaarnu / v. improve
sudhaar / n. improvement
suddhi / n. sense
sudho / n. adj. simple; innocent
sujhaab / n. suggestion
suga / n. parrot
sugandha / n. smell (pleasant)
sukaaunu / v. dry
sukh / n. happiness; comfort
sukshma / adj. small
sukuti / n. dried meat

sulto / adj. right side up
sumpanu / v. hand over
sun / n. gold
sunaulo / adj. golden
sunaar / n. goldsmith
sungur / n. pig
sunnu / v. hear
sunsaan / adj. n. quiet
suntalaa / n. mandarin orange
surakshya / n. security
surung / n. tunnel
surya / n. sun
sushil / adj. well mannered
suskeraa / n. sigh
susta / adj. slow
sutkeri / adj. woman immediately after childbirth
sutnu / v. sleep
swabhaab / n. nature
swaabhaabik / adj. natural
swaad / n. taste
swaadista / adj. tasty

swaagat / n. welcome
swaami / n. master; husband; holy man
swaang / n. pretence
swaartha / n. self-interest
swaarthi / n. adj. selfish
swaasthya / n. health
swaasni / n. wife
swadesh / n. one's own country
swadeshi / adj. belonging to one's own country
swarga / n. heaven
swastha / adj. n. healthy
swayambar / n. ceremony in which a girl chooses her husband
swatantra / adj. independent
swayam / n. oneself
swayattata / n. autonomy
swayamsewak / n. volunteer
sweekar / n. acceptance
sweekar garnu / v. accept
syaahaar / n. care
syaal / n. jackal

syaau / n. apple

taachhnu / v. scrap

taaja / adj. n. fresh

taajubee / n. surprise

taakat / n. power; strength

taaknu / v. aim

taakuraa / n. peak

taal / n. lake

taalchaa / n. lock

taalim / n. training

taamaa / n. copper; bamboo shoots

taangaa / n. horse driven carriage

taangnu / v. hang

taannu / v. pull

taansnu / v. stick

taap / n. heat

taapke / n. frying pan

taapkram / n. temperature

taapnu / v. warm by fire

taapu / n. island

taar / n. telegram

taaraa / n. star
taadhaa / adv. far
taarikh / n. date
taariph / n. praise
taarnu / v. get across rive
taash / n. playing cards
taato / adj. hot
taatparya / n. meaning
taba / adv. then
tadbhab / words borrowed by Nepali language with change
tagaaro / n. obstacle
tahalnu / n. stroll; walk
tai pani / in spite of
taiyaar / adj. ready
takkar / n. collision
takliph / n. trouble
takmaa / n. medal
tala / adv. below
talaak / n. divorce
talaashi / n. search

tamaashaa / n. spectacle

talab / n. salary

talkanu / v. shine

tallo / adj. lower

tamaatar / n. tomato

tamaam / adj. entire; whole

tambu / n. tent

tan / n. body

tanneri / n. youth

tapaai / pron. you

tapari / n. plate made of leaves

tapasyaa / n. meditation

tara / conj. but

taaraa / n. star

tarai / n. lowlands in the south of Nepal

taraaju / n. scale

tarkaari / n. vegetable

tarwaar / n. sword

tarkaa / n. method; way

tarsanu / v. be afraid

tarul / n. yam

tasbeer / n. photo; picture

tataaunu / v. heat

tathya / adj. actual; true

tatkaalin / adj. contemporary

tatsam / n. words borrowed in Nepali without modification

taul / n. weight

tebaa / n. support

teknu / v. step on

tel / n. oil

thaaknu / v. get tired

thaal / n. dish used for food

thaali / n. dish containing variety of food

thaalu / n. elder

thaanaa / n. police station

thaant / n. showing off; decoration

thaaun / n. place

thag / n. cheat

thagi / v. cheating

thahaa / n. knowledge

thaili / n. small bag

thakkar / n. collision

thakkar khaanu / v. collide

thakaai / n. fatigue

thakaali / n. tribe living in the hills of west Nepal

thankyaaunu / v. put away

thap / adj. additional

thappar / n. slap

thataaunu / v. beat

thatta / n. joke

thekedaar / n. contractor

thelnu / v. push

thekka / n. contract

thik / n. correct

thiti / n. young girl

thito / n. young boy

thoknu / v. strike

thorai / adj. little

thotro / adj. old; worn out

thuk / n. spite

thulo / adj. n. big

thunaa / n. arrest

thunnu / v. arrest

thupro / adj. a lot; pile

thupka / n. tibetan soup

thutnu / v. snatch

tihaar / five day festival in November

tij / n. festival in September for women

tika / n. red mark put on forehead

tikho / adj. sharp

tilahari / n. gold neckless worn by married women

timi / pron . you (used for children and some close friends)

tira / prep. towards

tiraskaar / n. abuse

tirtha / n. pilgrimage

tirthayaatri / n. pilgrim

tithi / n. day used in lunar calendar

tito /daj. bitter

toknu / v. bite

tol / n. locality

toophaan / n. storm

top / n. cannon

topi / n. cap

todnu / v. break

tolaaunu / v. stare

trishul / n. trident

tirishuli / n. name of river in west Nepal

tuhuro / n. adj. orphan

tunginu / v. end

tuppa / n. top

tutnu / n. break

tyaag / n. renouncement

tyasto / in that manner

tyati / that much

tyatro / as big as

tyo / pron. he; she; it; that

u / pron. he

ubhinu / v. stand up

ubhyaunu / v. erect

ubjani / n. crop; produce

ubjaau / adj. fertile

ubjaaunu / v.grow

uchchaaran / n. pronunciation

uchhinnu / v. overtake

uchit / adj. proper
udaan / n. flight
udaar / ajd. liberal
udaarbaad / n. liberalism
udaas / adj. sad
udaasi / n. sadness
udaya / n. rise
udan tashtari / n. flaying saucer
udar / n. stomach
uddeshya / n. objective
uddhaar / n. salvation
uddharan / n. extract
udghaatan / n. inauguration
udnu / v. fly
udus / n. bed bug
udyaan / n. garden
udyog / n. industry
ughaarnu / v. open
ugrabaad / n. extremism
ugrabaadi / n. extremist
uhi / adj. same

uhile / adv. past
ujaad / n. barren
ujur / n. complaint
ukaalo / n. climb; rise; steep gradient
ukhaan / n. proverb
ukhelnu / v. uproot
ukusmukus / n. soffocation
ukhu / n. sugar cane
ullekh / n. mention; description
ultaa / n. opposite
umaalnu / v. boil
umedbaar / n. candidate
umer / n. age
umkinu / v. get away
umlanu / v. boil
umranu / v. grow
un / n. wool
unchaai / n. height
uncho / adj. high; tall
uni / pron. he/she
uniharu / pron. they

unnat / adj. high yielding; developed
unnati / n progress
unt / n. camel
upaadhi / n. title
upa / n. assistant; vice
upa-baas / n. fasting
upadesh / n. preaching
upadrab / n. michief
upadro / n. mischief
upahaar / n. gift
upahaas / n. ridicule
upakar / n. welfare; charity
upakaari / adj. benevolent
upalabdhi / n. achievement
upamaa / n. anology
upanibesh / n. colony
upanyaas / n. novel
upasthit / n. present
upatyakaa / n. valley
upaaya / n. method
upayog / n. use

upayogi / adj. useful
upayogita / adj. utility
upayukta / adj. appropriate
upiyaa / n. flea
uphrinu / v. jump
urjaa / n. energy
ushaa / n. dawn
usto / adv. as; same as before
utaa / adv. there
utaarnu / v. take down; bring down
uthaaunu / v. raise; collect
utpaadan / n. production
utpaat / n. disaster
utrinu / v. descent
utsab / n. festival
utsuk / adj. anxious
uttam / adj. good quality
uttar / n. north; answer
uttaraadhikaari / n. successor
uttardaai / adj. responsible
uttejanaa / n. excitement

uttejit / adj. excited

uttinkhera / at the same time

waakka hunu / v. be fed up

waari / this side of river

waaris / n. legal representative in a suit

waastaa / n. concern

wahaan / pron . he (polite)

wajan / n. weight

wakil / n. lawyer

wara / adj. near

watan / n. residence; address

yaa / conj. or

yaad / n. memory

yahaan /adv. here

yaam / n. season

yaataayat / n. transport

yaatraa / n. journey

yaatri / n. traveller

yahudi / n. jew

yasari / adv. thus

yash / n. fame

yataa / adv. here; this way
yathaartha / adj. actual
yati / as many as this
yatro / as big as this
yaun / n. sex
yaun rog / n. veneral disease
yi / pron. these
yini / pron . he; she
yiniharu / pron. they
yo / pron. he; she; it
yog / n. meditation
yogi / n. one who practices yoga
yogya / adj. worthy; qualified
yogyataa / n. qualification
yoni / n. female sexual organ

ENGLISH-NEPALI

a / ek
abandon / v. chhodnu
abduct / v. bhagaaunu; apaharan garnu
abduction / n. apaharan
able / adj. samartha, laayak, garna sakne
ability / n. saamarthya
abnormal / n. asaadhaaran
abode / n. ghar; aabaas
aboriginal / n. aadibaasi
about / prep. maathi
about / adv. lagbhag
above / prep. maathi
abroad / adv. bidesh
abrupt / adj. ekaek, akasmaat
absent / gayal, anupasthit
absorb / v. linu
abundant / adj. dherai, prasasta
abuse / v. gaali garnu
accord / n. samjhauta
account / n. hisaab
accident / n. durghatana

accurate / adj. theek; baastabik
accuse / v. dosh lagaaunu
ache / dukhne
achieve / v. paaunu
action / n. kaam
acquaintance / chineko maanchhe
acquire / v. paaunu
across / adv. paari
add / v. jodnu
addition / n. thap; jodne
address / n. thegaana
adequate / adj. prasasta
admission / bharnaa; prabesh
administration / n. prashaasan
admit / v. pasna dinu; mannu
adultery / n. jaari
advance (money) / n. peshgi
advantage / n. laabh, phaida
adventure / n. saahasko kaam
adversary / n. pratidwandi
advertisement / n. bigyaapan

advice / n. sallaha
advise / v. sallah dinu
advisor / n. sallahkaar
aeroplane / hawaai jahaaj
affair / n. kuro
affection / n. maaya; sneh
affiliate / adj. sambandha bhaeko
affluent / adj. dhani
afford / v. kharcha garna saknu
afraid / v. daraaunu
after / prep. pachhi
afternoon / n. diuso
again / adv. pheri
agenda / n. chhalphal ko bisaya
agent / n. pratinidhi
agree / v. maannu
agriculture / n. krishi
aid / n. sahaayata; sahayog
aim / n. uddyeshya
air / n. haawa
airport / n. hawaai addaa

alcohol / n. raksi
alert / n. saabadhaan; hoshiyaar
alien / adj. bidheshi
alike / adj. ustai; eknaasko
alive / adj. baacheko; jiundo
all / n. sab; jammai
all at once / sab ek choti
all of us / haami sabai
all over / sabai tira
ally / n. mitra
allow / v. garna dinu
almanac / n. paatro
alomnd / n. badaam
almost / adv. jhandai
alphabet / akshar
already / adv. agaadi nai
also / adv. pani, samet
although / bhaepani
altitude / uchaai
altogether / adv. sangai. jammai
always / adv. sadhai

ambassador / n. rajdoot
ameliorate / v. sudhaar garnu
ammunition / n. gola barood
among / prep. madhye
ample / prasasta
ancestor / purukhaa
ancient / puraano, pracheen
and / cong. ra; au
anger / ris; krodh
angry / risaeko
animal / janaawar
annual / baarshik
another / adj. arko
answer / n. jawab; uttar
ant / kamilaa
anthropology / maanab shastra
anxiety / chintaa; phikri
anxious / adj. utsuk; chintit
any / adj. kunai; kohi
anyone / pron. josukai
anyway / adv. je bhae pani

apart / adv. beglai

apologize / v. maaphi maagnu

appear / v. dekhinu

appetite / bhok

apple / syau

application / aabedan, darkhasta

apply / v. darkhasta (aabedan) haalnu

appoint / v. niyukta garnu

appointment / niyukti, bhetghatko samaya

appreciate / v. kadar garnu

approach / v. najik jaanu

appropriate / suhaaudo

approval / sweekriti

approximate / andaaji; pug napug; karib

apricot / khurpani

aptitude / abhiruchi

area / chhetra

argue / v. bahas garnu

argument / bahas; chhalphal

arid / sukkha

arise / v. uthnu

arm / haat
army / senaa
around / prep. waripari; karib
arouse / v. uthaaunu
arrange / v. bandobasta garnu
arrangement / prabandha, bandobasta
arrest / v. samaatnu; pakranu
arrive / v. aaipugnu
arrogant / adj. ghamandi; abhimaani
art / n. kalaa
artist / n. kalaakar
article / n. bastu; cheej; lekh
ascent / n. chadhaai
asleep / adv. nidaaeko
as / adv. jasto
ass / gadhaa
ashamed / adj. laaj laageko
aside / adv. ekaatira
assault / hamalaa
assemble / v. to gather
assembly / n. sabha

assist / v. sahaayata garnu
assistance / sahaayataa
asylum / n. sharan
at / prep. ma
atheist / n. naastik
atmosphere / n .bayumandal
attach / sangai raakhnu
attempt / n. koshis; prayas
attempt / v. koshis garnu, prayaas garnu
attention / dhyaan
attitude / manobritti
attorney / n. wakil, adhibaktaa
attraction / n. aakarshan
auction / n. leelam
audit / n. lekhaa parikshan
auditor / n. lekha parikshak
author / n. lekhak
authority / adhikaar
automatic / aaph se aaph
auxillary / sahaayak
avenue / n. bato; sadak

average / saala khaala; sardar
avoid / v. chhalnu
awake / utheko; jaageko
await / v. parkhanu
award / n. purashkaar
awkward / apthyaro laagne
away / taadhaa
axe / n. bancharo
baby / n. bachchaa
bachelor / n. abibaahit; kumar
back / n. pachhaadi
backbiting / n. pachhadi kuraa katne
background / n. prishtabhumi
backing / n. samarthan
backward / adj. pichhadieko
bad / adj. kharaab; naraamro
bag / n. jholaa; thailee
bail / n. jamaani
balance / n. baanki (account); taraaju
bangle / n. churaa
bank / n. byaank

bandit / n. daaku
bargain /n. sasto molko maal
bargain / v. moltol garnu
basis / n. aadhaar
basic needs / n. aadhaarbhut aabashayaktaa
basket / n. tokari
bat / n. chamero
battle / n. ladaai
be / v. hunu
beach / n. kinaaraa
bean / n. simi
bear / n. bhaalu
bear / v. sahanu
beard / n. daari
beast / n. pashu; jaanwar
beat / v. kutnu; pitnu
beautiful / adj. raamro; sundar
because / conj. kinabhane
become / v. hunu
bed / n. bichhaunaa; khaat
bedding / n. bistaraa; ochchhyan

bee / n. maahuri
beef / n. gaaiko masu
before / adv. agaadi
behaviour / n. byabahaar
beg / v. maagnu
beggar / n. maagne
begin / v. shuru garnu
beginning / n. shuru
behaviour / n. byabahaar
behind / adv. pachhaadi
belief / n. biswass
believe / v. biswaas garnu
beloved / adj. pyaaro
below / adv. tala
belt / n. petee
benefit / n. laabh; phaaida; hit
beside / adv. najikma; ko chheu maa
best / adj. sab bhandaa raamro
bet / n. baaji
bet / v. baaji thoknu
better / adj. jhan raamro

betray / v. dhokaa dinu
betrayal / n. dhokaa
between /adv. bichmaa; maajhmaa
beyond / adv. taadhaa ma
bias / n. anyaaya; paskshyapaat
big / adj. thulo
binocular / n. durbin
biography / n. jeewani
bird / n. charo
birth/ n. janma
birthday / n. janmadin; janmotsab
birthplace /n. janmasthal; janmabhoomi
bite / v. toknu
bitter / adj. tito
black / adj. kaalo
blacksmith / n. kaami
blame / v. dosh lagaaunu
blanket / n. kambal
blessing / n. aashirbaad
blind / n. andho
blood / n. ragat

blouse / n. cholo
blow / n. dhakkaa
blue / adj. neelo
bluff / n. dhokaa
bluff / v. dhokaa dinu
blunder / n. thulo bhool
boast / v. ghamanda garnu
boat / n. dungaa
body / n. shareer
bodyguard / n. angarakshak
boil / v. umalnu
boiled / adj. umaaleko (water); usineko (egg)
bone / n. haddi
book / n. kitaab; pustak
border / n. seemaanaa
borrow / v. saapat linu; rin linu
both / adj. dubai
bother / v. dukkha dinu
bottle / n. sisi
bottom / n. tala
boundary / n. seemaanaa

box / n. baakas
boy / n. ketaa; thitaa
brain / n. magaj
brave / adj. bahaadur
bread / n. roti; pauroti
break / v. bhaachnu
breathe / v. saas phernu
breakfast / n. bihaanako khaana
brick / n. int
bride / n. dulahi
bridge / n. pool
bright / adj. chamkilo
brief / adj. chhoto; samkshipta
bring / v. lyaaunu
broad / adj. chaudaa
broadcast / v. prasaaran garnu
broker / n. dalaal
brother / n. daaju; bhaai
brotherhood / n. bhraatritwa
brother-in-law / n. saalo; jethaan; juwaai
brown / adj. khairo

brutal / adj. nirdayi
budget / n. bajet; aaya-byaya bibaran
build / b. banaaunu
buffalo / n. raango; bhainsi
bullock / n. goru
burden / n. bojh; bhaari
burglar / n. chor
burn / v. balnu
bus / n. bas
business / n. byaapaar; dhandaa
busy / adj. byasta
but / conj. tara
butcher / n. kasaai
butter / n. makkhan
butterfly / n. putali
buy / v. kinnu
by / prep. najik; baata
cabbage / n. bandaagobhi
cabinet / n. mantrimandal
calculate / v. hisaab garnu; gannu
calendar / n. bhitte patro

calf / n. baachcho
calm / adj. shaanta
camel / n. unt
camera / n. kyaameraa
can / v. saknu
canal / n. nahar
candidate / n. ummedbaar
candle / main batti
cap / n. topi
capable / adj. yogya; samarthya
capital / n. raajdhaani; punji
capitalism / n. punjibaad
captain / n. kaptaan
car / n. kaar
care / v. herbichaar garnu; dhyaan dinu
careful/ adj. saabadhaan; hoshiyaar
carpenter / n. karmi
carpet / n. galaichaa
carry / v. boknu; lagnu
carrot / n. gaajar
cash / n. nagad

caste / n. jaat

cat / n. biraalo

catch / v. samaatnu

cattle / n. gaaigoru

caution / n. saabadhaani

cave / n. gufaa

cement / n. simanti

census / n. janagananaa

center / n. kendra; beech; madhya

central / adj. kendriya

cereal / n. anna

ceremony / n. samaaroha

certain / adj. kehi

certificate / n. pramaan patra

chair / n. kursi

character / n. charitra

characteristic / n. bisheshataa

chase / v. lakhetnu

cheap / adj. sasto

cheat / v. thagnu

check / v. jaanch garnu

cheerful / adj. prasanna, khushi bhaeko
chest / n. chhati
chicken / n. kukhuraa
chief / n. mukhya
child / n. bachchaa; ketaaketi
chilly / n. khursaani
choose / v. chhannu
chose / adj. chhaneko
citizen / n. naagarik
citizenship / n. naagariktaa
city / n. nagar; shahar
civilization / n. sabhyataa
civilized / adj. sabhya
claim / v. daabi garnu; n. daabi
class / n. klas; kakshyaa
clay / n. maato
clean / adj. saphaa
clear / adj. spasta
clever / adj. chalaak
climate / n. haawaa paani; jalbaayu
climb / v. chadhnu

clock / n. ghadi
close / v. banda garnu
closed / adj. banda
cloth /n. luga; kapadaa
cloud / n. baadal
coal / n. koilaa
coat / n. kot
coffee / n. kafi
coin /n. paisaa; sikkaa
cold / n. adj. chiso; jaado
collect / v. jamma garnu
colony / n. upanibesh
come / v. aaunu
comfort / n. subistaa
commerce / n. baanijya
committee / n. samiti
common / adj. saadhaaran; maamuli; saajhaa
communication / n. sanchaar
comparision / n. tulanaa
compensation / n. muaabajaa; kshyatipurti
competent / adj. yogya

competition / n. pratiyogitaa; pratispardhaa

complain / v. ujur garnu; chitta nabujeko kuraa garnu

complete / adj. pooraa

complete / v. pooraa garnu

complicated / adj. kathin; gaahro

compulsary / adj. anibarya

concern / n. matlab; waastaa

concerning / prep. baaremaa

conduct / n. chaalchalan

confidence / n. chaalchalan

confidence / n. biswaas

confuse / v. almalinu

confusion / n. almal

congratulate / v. badhaai dinu

congratulations / n. badhaai; abhinandhan

connection / n. sambandha

conquest / n. bijaya; jitnu

consent / n. sweekriti

consider / v. bichaar garnu

considerable / adj. nikai

constitution / n. sambidhaan

construct / v. banaaunu
construction / n. nirmaan
contact / n. samparka
continue / v. kaam gariraakhnu
control / n. niyantran
convenient / adj. subidhaajanak
convince / v. biswass dilaaunu
cook / n. bhaanse
cool / adj. thandaa
co-operate / v. sahayog garnu
co-operation / n. sahayog
corn / n. anna
coronation / n. raajyaabhishek
corporation/ n. samsthaan; nigam
correct / adj. theek; shuddha
correct / v. shuddha garnu
correction / n. shuddhi
corrupt / adj. bhrasta
corruption / n. bhraachaachaar
cost / n. mol
costly / adj. mahango

cotton / adj. kapaas
council / n. parishad
count / v. gannu
counterfeit / n. jaali
country / n. desh
countryman /n. deshbaasi
courage / n. saahas
courageous / adj. saahasi
court / n. adaalat
courtesy / n. udaarata; shistaachaar
cover / v. dhaaknu
cow / n. gaai
coward / adj. laachhi; kaathar
crash / v. dhakka laagnu; durghatana parnu
crazy / adj. baulaaha; paagal
create / v. nirmaan garnu; sirjanaa garnu
creation / n. srishti; nirmaan
credit / n. saapati; udhaaro; jas
cremate /v. jalaaunu; daaha samskaar garnu
cremation /n. daaha samskaar
crime / n. aparaadh

criminal / n. aparaadhi

crisis / n. sankat

critic / n. samaalochak

criticism / n. samaalochanaa

criticize / v. aalochana garnu

crocodile / n. graaha

crook / n. badmaas; thag

crop / n. baali

cross / v. paar garnu

crowd / n. bheed; janasamuha

crown / n. shripech; raajmukut

crown prince / n. yubaraaj dhiraaj

cruel / adj. nirdayi

crush / v. dabaaunu

cry / v. runu; karaaunu

cuckoo / n. koili

cucumber / n. kaakro

culprit / n. doshi

cultivate / v. kheti lagaaunu

culture / n. samskriti

curd / n. dahi

cure / v. okhati hunu; niko hunu

current / adj. haalko; prachalit

curse / n. sraap

curtain / n. pardaa

cushion / n. takiyaa

custom / n. riti riwaaj; bhansaar

cut / v. kaatnu

daily / n. adj. dindinai; pratyek din

dairy / n. dugdha shaalaa

dam / n. baandh

damage / n. noksaan; haani

dance /n. naach

danger /n. khataraa

dangerous / adj. bhayankar

dark / n. andhakaar; andhyaaro

darn / v. raphu garnu

data / n. tathyaanka

date / n. taarikh; miti

daughter / n. chhori

daughter-in-law / n. buhaari

dawn / n. jhismise; bhor; ushaakaal

day / n. din
dead / adj. mareko
deaf / n. bahiro
deal / v. byabahaar garnu; byabasaaya garnu
dear / adj. pyaaro; priya
death / n. mrityu
debate / n. baad bibaad
debt / n. rin; saapati
decay / v. sadnu; naash hunu
deceive / v. thagnu; dhokaa dinu
decency / n. shistataa
decent / adj. shista; bhalaadmi
decide / v. nirnaya garnu
decision / n. nirnaya
decimal / n. dashamalab
declaration / n. ghoshanaa; bhanaai
decline / v. ghatnu
decrease / n. kami
decrease / v. ghatnu
dedication / n. samarpan
deduct / v. ghataaunu

deep / adj. gahiro
deer / n. mriga
defeat / n. haar; paraajaya
defeat / v. haraaunu
defect / n. dosh
defense / n. rakshyaa; bachaabat
deficiency / n. kami; apurnata
deficit / n. ghaata
definite / adj. nischit; pakkaa
delay / n. aber
delay / v. aber garnu
delete / v. hataaunu
delicate / adj. komal
delicious / adj. swaadishta; meetho
delighted / adj. prasanna
deliver / v. puryaaunu
demand / n. maang
demand / v. maagnu
democracy / n. prajaatantra; janatantra
democratic / adj. prajaataantrik
demon / n. raakshas

demonstrate / v. pramaan saath dekhaaunu

demonstration / n. pradarshan

denounce / v. gaali garnu; nindaa garnu

dental / adj. daant sambandhi

dentist / n. daant ko daaktar

deny / v. namaannu; asweekaar garnu

depart / v. jaanu; prasthaan garnu

department / n. bibhaag

departure / n. prasthaan

depend / v. nirbhar hunu

dependable / adj. patyaauna sakne

dependence / n. nirbharataa

deport / v. desh baahira nikaalnu

depth / n. gahiraai

descend / v. orlanu; tala jharnu

descent / n. orlaai

describe / v. bayaan garnu

description / n. barnan; bayaan

desert / n. marubhumi

deserve / v. yogya hunu

designation / n. pad; upaadhi

desire / n. ichchhaa

despair / n. niraashaa

destiny / n. bhaagya

destroy / v. naash garnu

detail / n. bibaran

detailed / adj. puraa bibaran saath

determine / v. pattaa lagaaunu

difference / n. pharak

different / adj. pharak; beglai; asamaan

difficult / adj. gaahro

difficulty / adv. kathinaai saath

difficulty / n. kathinaai

dig / v. khannu

digest / v. pachaaunu

diminish / v. ghatnu

dinner / n. belukaa ko khaanaa

diplomat /n. kutanitigya

diplomatic / adj. kutnitik

direct / adj. seedhaa

direction / n. dishaa

director / n. nirdehashak

directory / n. nirdeshikaa

dirt / n. mailo

dirty / adj. phohar

disadvantage / n. haani; bephaayadaa

disagree / v. namaannu

disappear / v. haraaunu

disappoint / v. niraash parnu

disaster / n. bipatti; barbaadi

disciple / n. chelaa; shisya

discipline / n. anushaasan

discovery / n. khoj; aabishkaar

discretion / n. bibek; saabadhaani

discrimination / n. bhed bhaab

discuss / v. chhalphal garnu

discussion / n. chhalphal

disease / n. rog

dishonest / adj. beimaan

dismiss / v. khaarej garnu; bidaa garnu

disorder / n. abyabasthaa

disparity / n. asamaanataa

distance / n. doori

distinguish / v. chhuttyaaunu
district / n. jillaa
disturb / v. khalbal garnu; baadhaa garnu
disturbance / n. khalbali; baadhaa
ditch / n. khaadal
diverse / adj. beglai; anek
divide / v. baadnu; bibhaajan garnu
division / n. bibhaajan
divorce / n. talaak
do / v. garnu
doctor / n. daaktar
dog / n. kukkur
doll / n. putali
domestic / n. gharaayasi; aantarik
domicile / n. niwaas
domination / n. shaasan
donation / n. chandaa
donkey / n. gadhaa
door / n. dhokaa
double / n. dui gunaa; dabal
doubt / n. shankaa; sandeha

down / adv. tala
downstairs / adv. tala
draw / v. taannu
dream / n. sapanaa
dress / n. lugaa
dress / v. lugaa lagaaunu
drink / v. piunu
drive / v. gaadi haaknu
drop / v. chhodnu
dry / adj. sukhaa
dubious / adj. shankaa laagne
due / n. tirna parne paisaa
dull / adj. bodho; manda buddhi
dump / v. phyaaknu
duplicate / n. pratilipi
durable / adj. tikaau
duration / n. awadhi
during / prep. abadhi maa
dust / n. dhulo
duty / n. kartabya
dwarf / n. baampudke

dwelling / n. basne ghar; niwaas
dye / n. rang
dysentry / n. aaun ragat
each / adj. harek; pratyek
eager / adj. utsuk
eagerly / adv. utsaah sahit
ear / n. kaan
early / adj. chaadai
earn / v. kamaaunu
ear ring / n. kaan paasaa
earth / n. prithbi; dharti
earthquake / n. bhukampa; bhainchaalo
easily / adv. sajilo sita
east / n. purba
eastern / adj. purbiya
easternmost / adj. sab bhandaa purba
easy / adj. sajilo; sugam
eat / v. khaanu
echo / n. pratidhwani
eclipse / n. grahan
economic / adj. aarthik

economics / n. arthashaastra

economist / n. arthashaastri

edit / v. sampaadan garnu

edition / n. samskaran

editor / n. sampaadak

editorial / n. sampaadakiya

education / n. sikshaa; padhaai

effect / n. asar

effective / adj. raamro asar parne; prabhaabkaari

effort / n. koshis; prayatna

egg / n. phul; andaa

either / adj. ki yo ki u; kita

elderly / adj. budho

eldest / n. jetho

elect / v. nirbaachit garnu

election / n. chunaab

electric / adj. bijuli sambandhi

electricity / n. bijuli

elementary / adj. praathamik; saamaanya

elephant / n. haatti

eliminate / v. hataaunu; jhiknu

else / adv. aru; atirikta
elsewhere / adv. anyatra; anta; aru thaaunmaa
emancipation / n. mukti
embarass / v. lajjit paarnu
embrace / n. aalingan
emerald / n. pannaa
emergency / n. aakasmik ghatanaa
emotion / n. bhaabanaa
emphasis / n. bishes dhyaan
emphasize / v. bishes dhyaan dinu
empire / n. saamraajya
employ / v. kaam lagaaunu; niyukta garnu
employment / n. rojgaar
empty / adj. khaali; shunya
enclose / v. banda garnu
encourage / v. protsaahit garnu
encouragement / n. protsaahan
encyclopedia / n. bishwakosh
end / n. anta
endeavour / n. prayatna
enemy / n. shatru

energy / n. urjaa; shakti

engineer / n. injiniar

english / n. angreji

englishman / n. angrej

enhance / v. badhaaunu

enjoy / v. upabhog garnu; aananda garnu

enjoyment / n. aananda; sukh

enormous / adj. bishaal

enough / n. paryaapta; pugdo

ensure / v. nischit garnu

enter / v. pasnu

entrance / n. pasne dhokaa; prabesh

entertain / v. aatithya garnu

entertainment / n. manoranjan

enthusiasm / n. utsaah

entire / n. sampoorna; puraa

entirely / adv. puraa roop le

envelope / n. khaam

envious / adj. irshyaa garne

envoy / n. kutnaitik pratinidhi; raajdoot

envy / n. daah; irshyaa

epic / n. mahaakaabya
epidemic / n. mahaamaari
equal / n. samaan; baraabar
equipment / n. saamaan
equitable / adj. nyaayochit
era / n. yug
eradication / n. unmoolan
erase / v. metnu
erect/ v. nirmaan garnu
error / n. bhool
escape / v. bhaagnu
especial / adj. bishista
espionage / n. jaasusi
essay / n. nibandha
essential / adj. bishista
establish / v. sthaampanaa garnu
estimate / n. anumaan
eternal / adj. ananta
ethnic / adj. jaatiya
evacuate / v. khaali garnu; nikaalnu
evaluation / n. mulyaankan

even / adv. bhaepani
evening / n. saanjh
event / n. ghatanaa
ever / adv. sadhai
everybody / n. sabijanaa
everyday / adj. pratidin
everywhere / adv. sabai thaaunmaa
evidence / n. pramaan
evident / adj. spasta
evil / adj. kharaab
exact / adj. yathaartha; theek
exactly / adv. theek
exaggerate / v. badhaaera bhannu
examination / n. jaanchnu
examine / v. jaanchnu
example / n. udaaharan
excellent / adj. atyuttam
except / prep. baahek
exception / n. apabaad
excess / n. atibadhi
exchange / n. binimaya

exchange / saatnu
excise / n. antashulka
excite / v. aabeshma lyaaunu
excitement / n. uttejanaa
excursion / n. ghumphir; bhraman
excuse / v. maaph garnu
execute / v. praan danda dinu;
kaaryaanban garnu
exercise / n. byaayaam; abhyaas
exhausting / adj. thakaaune
exist / v. rahanu
expect / v. aashaa garnu
expert / n. bisheshagya
expense / n. kharcha
expensive / adj. mahango
experience / n. anubhab
experiment / n. prayog
explain / v. bayaan garnu; bujhaaunu
explanation / n. byaakhyaa
exploitation /n. shoshan
explore / v. khojnu

explosive / n. bisphotak

export / n. niryaat; nikaasi

expose / v. dekhaaidinu; bhandaaphod garnu

express / v. byakta garnu

extend / v. phailaaunu

extensive / adj. bistrit

extent / n. seemaa

exterior / n. baahiri bhaag

external / adj. baahiri

extinguish / v. nibhaaunu

extort / v. dhutnu

extra / adj. badhi

extra-ordinary / adj. asaadhaaran

extravagant / adj. phajulkharchi

extremely / adv. atyanta

extremist / n. aatankabaadi

eye / n. aankhaa

eyewitness / n. pratyakshadarshi

face / n. mukh; anuhaar

facility / n. subidhaa

fact / n. saancho kuraa; satya kuraa

factory / n. kaarkhaanaa

fail / v. asaphal hunu

failure / n. asaphalataa

faint / n. murchhaa

fair / n. melaa

faith / n. biswaas

faithful / adj. biswasniya

fall/ v. khasnu

false / adj. jhuto

fame / n. yash

familiar / adj. parichit; raamrari chineko

family / n. paribaar

famine / n. anikaal

famous / adj. prasiddha

fan / n. pankhaa

fanatic / n. dharma maa kattar

fancy / n. kalpanaa

far / n. taadhaa

fare / n. bhaadaa

farm / n. khet

farmer / n. khetiwaal; krishak

farming / n. kheti; krishi

fascinating / adj. ramaailo; manmohak

fascist / n. taanaashah

fast / v. upabaas basnu; brata garnu

fast / adv. chaado

fat / n. moto

fate / n. bhaagya

father / n. baabu; pita

father-in-law / n. sasuraa

fatigue / n. thakaai

fault / n. dosh

faulty / adj. doshpurna; asuddha

favour / n. anugraha

favourite / n. adj. manpareko

fear / n. dar

fearful / adj. darlaagne; bhayankar

feasibility / n. sambhaabyata

feast / n. bhoj

feature / n. aakaar; lakshan

federal / adj. sanghiya

fee / n. shulka; phis

feel / v. anubha garnu; laagnu

feeling / n. bhaabanaa

fellow / n. saathi

felon / n. aparaadhi

female / n. aaimaai; mahilaa

fertile / adj. upjaau

festival / n. chaahaad; jaatraa; utsab

feudal / adj. saamanti

fever / n. jaro; jwar

few / n. kehi

fiction / n. kalpanaa

fictitious / adj. kaalpanik

field / n. karyakshetra

fierce / adj. bhayankar

fighting / n. ladaai; yuddha

fill / b. bharnu

filthy / adj. phohar

final / adj. antim; aakhiri

finance / n. artha; bitta

finance minister / n. artha mantri

find / v. paaunu; bhettaunu

fine / n. danda; jariwaanaa

fine arts / n. lalit kalaa

finger /n. aunlo

finish / v. siddhinu

fire / n. aago

fire brigade / n. damkal

firewood / n. daauraa

first / n. adj. pahilo; pratham

first class / adj. pratham shreni

fish / n. maachhaa

fitting / n. yogya

flag / n. jhandaa

flat / n. chepto

flavor / n. swaad; sugandha

flight / n. udaan

flirt / v. jiskanu

flood / n. baadhi

flour / n. pitho

flow / v. bahanu

flower / n. phool

fluctuate / v. tala maathi garnu

fluent / adj. raamrari bolne

fly / v. udnu

fog / n. tusaaro; hussu

follow / v. pachhi laagnu; bujhnu

follower / n. chelo; anuaayi

following / adj. nimnalikhit

food / n. khaanaa; khaanekuraa

fool / n. murkha

foot / n. khutta

for / prep. nimti; nimitta; ko laagi

forbidden / adj. manaai gareko; garna napaaine

force / n. shakti; bal

forced / adj. jabarjasti

forecast / n. bhabisyabaani

forefather / n. purukhaa; baabubaaje; purbaj

foreign / adj. bideshi

foreigner / n. bideshi

foreign minister / n. pararaashtra mantri

forest / n. ban; jangal

forgery / n. kirte

forget / v. birsanu

forgive / v. maaph garnu
formality / n. aupachaariktaa
former / adj. bhutapurba
fort / n. killaa
fortnight / n. dui haptaa
forunate / adj. bhaagyamaani
fortunately / adv. saubhaagyabash
fortune / n. bhaagya
fortune-teller / n. jyotishi
forward / n. agaadi
foundation / n. jag; aadhaarshilaa
frank / adj. spastha baktaa
free / adj. swatantra
freeze / v. jamnu
frequent / adj. aksar
fresh / adj. taajaa
friend / n. saathi; mitra
friendship / n. mitrataa
frontier / n. seemaa
frost / n. tusaaro
fruit / n. phalphul

fry / v. taarnu; bhutnu
fuel / n. indhan
full / adj. puraa
fun / n. majaa; ramaailo
fund / n. kosh
fundamental / adj. aabashyak; maulik
funeral / n. antim samskaar
furious / adj. dherai risaaeko
future/ n. bhabisya
gain / n. laabh; phaaidaa
gamble / n. juwaa
gamble / v. juwaa khelnu
game / n. khel
gangster / n. badmaas
garage / n. gyarej
garden / n. bagaichaa; baari
gardener / n. maali
garland / n. maalaa
garlic / n. lasun
garment / n. lugaa; bastra
gate / n. dhokaa; dwaar

gather / v. jammaa garnu

gazette / n. rajpatra

gem / n. ratna

gender / n. linga

general / n. senaapati

general / adj. saadhaaran

generally / adv. saadhaaran ruple

generosity / n. udaarataa

generous / adj. udaar; daanshil

gentle / adj. bhalaadmi, shaanta

gentleman / n. bhalaadmi, bhadra byakti

genuine / adj. baastabik; pramaanik

geography / n. bhugol

geology / n. bhugarbha   shaastra

germ / n. keetaanu

get / v. paaunu, linu

get out / v. baahira jaanu

get up / v. uthnu

get to know / v. parichaya hunu; chinnu

ghost / n. bhut; pret

gift / n. daan; upahaar

ginger / n. aduwaa

girl / n. keti; thiti

give / v. dinu

give up / v. chhodnu

glacier / n. himanadi

glad / adj. prasanna; khushi

glass / n. kaach

glimpse / n. jhalak

globe / n. prithbi

glove / n. panjaa

go / v. jaanu

goal / n. lakshya; uddeshya

god / n. bhagawaan; ishwar

goddess / n. debi

gold / n. sun

golden / adj. sunaulaa

good / adj. asal; upayogi

good for nothing / adj. kaam na laagne

gossip / n. gaph

govern / v. saashan garnu

goverment / n. sarkaar

governmental / adj. sarkaari

graduate / adj. snaatak

gradual / adj. bistaarai

grammar / n. byaakarna

grand / adj. thulo; bishaal

grandfather / n. baaje; pitaamaha

grandson /n. naati

grant / n. daan; sahaayata

grass / n. ghaas

grateful / adj. kritagya

grave / n. chihaan

grave / adj. gambhir

graze / v. charnu

great / adj. bishaal; thulo; mahaa

greed / n. lobh; laalach

greedy / n. lobhi

green / adj. hariyo

greet / v. swaagat garnu

greeting / n. abhibaadan

grey / adj. khairo

grief / n. shok; dukkh

grilled / adj. sekeko
ground / n. jameen; bhain
growth / n. briddhi
guard / n. paale, chaukidaar
guardian / n. samrakshak
guava / n. ambaa
guess / v. anumaan garnu
guest / n. paahunaa; atithi
guide / n. patha pradarshak
guide / v. baato dekhaaunu
guilt / n. dosh
guilty / adj. doshi; aparaadhi
gum / n. gund
gun / n. bandook
gut / n. saahas
gutter / n. naali
gymnasium / n. byaayaamshaala
gynecologist / n. strirog bisheshagya
gynecology / n. strirog bigyaan
habit / n. baani
hair / n. kapaal

half / n. adj. aadhaa
half past / n. aadhaa ghanta pachhi; saadhe
half yearly / adj. ardha baarshik
hall / n. thulo kothaa
ham / n. sungur ko masu
hand / n. haat
handful / n. alikati
handicap / n. baadhaa
handkerchief / n. rumaal
happening / n. ghatanaa
happily / adv. bhaagyabash; aanandale
happiness /n. aananda; sukh
happy / adj. prasanna; sukhi
harrass / v. dukkha dinu
harbor / n. bandargaah
hard / adj. kadaa
harm / n. haani; noksaani
harmful / adj. haanikaarak
harvest / n. phasal
haste / n. hatpat
hastily / adv. hatpat sita

hat / n. top
hate / n. ghin; ghrinaa
hatred / n. ghrinaa
haunted / adj. bhut laagne
have / v. sanga hunu
havoc / n. biddhwamsa
hazard / n. sankat; khataraa
he / pron. u; tyo; uni
head / n. taauko
headache / n. taauko dukhne
headmaster / n. pradhaan adhyaapak
headquarters / n. pradhan kaaryaalaya
heal / v. niko hunu
health / n. swaastha
healthy / adj. nirogi
hear / v. sunnu
heart / n. mutu; hridaya
heat / n. taato; garmi
heaven / n. swarga
heavy / adj. garaun
height / n. unchaai

heir / n. uttaraadhikaari; hakbaalaa

hell / n. narak

help / n. sahaayataa

help / v. sahaayataa garnu; madad garnu

helpful / adj. sahaayata dine, madad dine

helpless / adj. asahaaya

henceforth / adv. aajadekhi

her / pron. usko

herd / n. bathaan

here / adv. yahaan

herewith / adv. yo sangain

heritage / n. purkhauli sampatti

hero / n. beer

hestitate / v. hichkichaaunu

heterogeneous / adj. bibhinna kisimko

hidden / adj. lukeko

hide / n. chhalaa

hide / v. lukaaunu

high / adj. aglo; uncho

highway / n. raajmaarga

hill / n. pahaad

hillock / n. saano pahaad; daandaa

hinder / v. baadhaa dinu

hinduism / n. hindu dharma

hint / n. sanket

hire / v. bhaadaamaa linu

his / pron. usko

historian / n. itihaaskaar

history / n. itihaas

hit / v. pitnu

hoard / v. jamaa garnu

hobby / n. man parkeo kuraa

hold / n. prabhaab

hold / v. samaatnu

hole / n. pwaal

holiday / n. bidaa

hollow / adj. khokro

holy / n. pabitra

home / n. ghar

homeland / n. swadesh

homemade / adj. gharmaa banaaeko

homesick / adj. ghar samjheko

honest / adj. imaandaar

honey / n. maha

honorarium / n. dakshinaa

honor / n. maan; aadar

honorable / adj. aadaraniya

hope / n. aashaa

hopeful / adj. aashaa garne

hopeless / adj. kaam nalaagne

horn / n. sing

horoscope / n. chinaa

horrible / adj. dar laagne; bhayankar

horticulture / n. phalodyaan; baaghbaani

hospital / n. aspataal

hospitality / n. atithisatkaar

hot / adj. taato

hour / n. ghantaa

house / n. ghar

housewife / n. grihini

how / adv. kasari

huge / adj. thulo

human / n. maanis

human rights / n. maanab adhikaar

humble / adj. saadhaaran; maamuli

humiliate / v, apmaan garnu

humourous / adj. hansilo

hunger / n. bhok

hungerstrike / n. anashan

hungry / adj. bhoko

hunting / n. shikaar

hurry / n. hatpat

hurt / v. chot lagaaunu

husband / n. logne

hydro-electric/ adj. jala bidyut

hydrology / n. jalasrot bigyaan

hypocrite / n. paakhandi

i /pron. ma

ice / n. hiun; baaarph

ice cream / n. aais kreem

idea / n. bichaar

ideal / n. aadarsha

ideally / adv. aadarasha roopmaa

identical /adj. durusta; ustai

identification / n. parichaya

identify / v. chinaaunu

idiot / n. murkha

idle / adj. alchhi

idol / n. murti

if / conj. yadi

ignorance / n. agyaanataa

ignorant / adj. najanne; thaaha nabhaeko

ill / n. biraami

illegal /adj. gair kaanuni; abaidh

illness / n. rog

illustrate / v. udaaharan dinu

ill-will /n. shatrutaa

image / n. murti

imaginary / adj. kaalpanik

imagination /n. kalpanaa

imitate / v. nakkal garnu

immature /adj. kaancho; paripakwa na bhaeko

immediate / adj. turunta

immediately / adv. turunta

immense / adj. thulo

immerse / v. dubaaunu
immigrant / n. aaprabaasi
immigration / n. aaprabaas deshaantarbaas
immoral / adj. byabhichaari
immortal / adj. amar
immovable / adj. achal
immunity / n. haani baata bachaaw
impatient / n. adhir; sahana na sakne
impediment / n. baadhaa
imperfect / adj. apurna; apuro
imperialism / n. saamraajyabaad
implement / n. saamaan; upakaran
implementation / n. kaaryaanwaban
import / n. .ahat
important / adj. mahatwapurna
importance / n. mahatwa
impossible / adj. asambhab
impress / v. prabhaab parnu
impression / n. prabhaab
impressive / adj. prabhaabshaali
imprint / n. chhaap

improper / adj. anuchit

improve / v. sudhrinu

improvement / n. sudhaar

impure / adj. apabitra

in / prep. baata; adv. bhitra

inability / n. asamathataa

inaccessible / adj. durgam

inaccurate / adj. asuddha

inactive / adj. alchhi; niskriya

inadequate / adj. aparyaapta; napug

inauguration / n. udhghaatan

incalculable / adj. anaginti

incense / n. dhoop

incentive / n. preranaa; utsaaha

incest / n. haadnaata karani

incident / n. ghatanaa

incline / v. dhalkinu

include / v. milaaunu; sammilit garnu

included / adj. sammilit; milaaeko

income / n. aamdaani; aaya

income tax / n. aaya kar

incomparable / adj. atulaniya

incompatible / adj. bipareet; namilne

incompetent / adj. ayogya

incomprehensible / adj. bujhna na sakne

inconvenience / n. asubidhaa

incorrect / adj. asuddha

increase / v. badhnu

incredible / adj. abishwasaniya

incurable / adj. asaadhya; niko na hune

indecent / adj. ashista

indeed / adv. baastabmaa

independence / n. swatantrataa

independent / adj. swatantra

independently / adv. swatantrataa sita

india / n. bhaarat

indicate / v. dekhaaunu; prakat garnu

indifference / n. udaasinataa; bewaastaa

indigestion / n. ajirna

indirect / adj. apraktyaksha

indispensable / adj. atyaabashyak; nabhai na hune

individual / n. byakti
individuality / n. byaktitwa
individually / adv. beglaa beglai
indoors / adj. gharbhitra
industrial / adj. audyogik
industrialist / n. udyog byabasaayi
industry / n. udhyog
ineffective / adj. nirathak
inefficient / adj. ayogya
ineligible / adj. lina na sakne
inevitable / adj. nabhai nahune; abashyambhaabi
inexperienced / adj. anubhabhin
infant / n. baalak; shishu
inferior / adj. ghatiyaa
inferiority / n. heenata
inflation / n. mudraa sphiti
influential / adj. prabhaabkaari
inform / v. suchanaa dinu; jaankaari dinu
informal / adj. anaupachaarik
information / n. jaankaari; suchanaa
inhabit / v. basnu

inhabitant / n. niwaasi; baasindaa

inhale / v. saas tannu

initial / adj. shuruko

injection / n. injekshan

injure / v. chot lagaaunu

injured / adj. ghaayal

injury / n. chot; ghaau

injustice / n. anyaaya

ink / n. masi

innermost / adj. sabbhandaa bhitrako

innocent / adj. niraparaadh

innumberable / adj. anaginti

inoculate / v. khopaaunu

inquire / v. sodhnu

inquiry / n. sodhpuchh

insane / adj. baulaahaa; paagal

insect / n. kiraa

insecure / adj. asurakshit

insert / v. ghusaaunu

inside / n. bhitra

insignificant / adj. saano; mahatwa nabhaeko

inspection / n. nirikshan
inspiration / n. preranaa
inspire / v. preranaa dinu; utsaaha dinu
instant / n. chhin
instantly / adv. turrunta
instead / adv. thaaunmaa
institute / n. samsthaa
instruct / v. sikshaa dinu
instruction / n. sikshaa; upadesh
insult / v. apamaan garnu
insult / n. apamaan; beijjati
insurance / n. beemaa
intellect / n. buddhi
intellectual / n. buddhijiwi
intelligent / adj. buddhimaan
intend / v. ichchha garnu
intention / n. ichchhaa
intercourse / n. sambandha; smabhog
interest / n. byaaj; chaakh; abhiruchi
interesting / adj. rochak; chaakhlagdo
interfere / v. roknu

interim / adj. antarim
interior / n. bhitri
intermarriage / n. antarjaatiya bibah
international / adj. antarraashtriya
interpret / v. artha lagaaunu
interpretation / n. byaakhyaa
interpretor / n. dobhaase; anubaad garne manchhe
intervene / v. beechmaa roknu
interview / n. antarbaartaa
intimacy / n. ghanista sambandha
intimidate / v. tarsaaunu
intolerable / adj. sahana na sakne
introduce / v. parichaya garaaunu
introduction /n. parichaya
introductary / adj. praarambhik
invade / v. hamalaa garnu; aakraman garnu
invent / v. aabiskaar garnu
invention / n. aabiskaar
invest / v. lagaani garnu
investigate / v. anusandhaan garnu; khoji garnu
investment /n. lagaani

invisible / adj. adrishya

invitation / n. nimtaa; nimantranaa

invite / v. nimtaa dinu; bolaaunu

iron / n. phalaam

iron / v. istri garnu

irregular / adj. aniyamit

irrigation / n. sinchaai

irritate / v. chidhaaunu; jharkinu

island / n. taapu

isolated / adj. eklieko

itching / n. chilaunu

itinerary / n. bhraman maarga

jackal / n. syaal

jail / n. jhyyaalkhaana; jel

janitor / n. chaukidaar; saphaai majdur

jar / n. ghadaa

jaundice / n. kamalpitta

jaw / n. daaraa

jealous / adj. daaha; irshyaa

jealousy / n. irshyaa

jeopardize / v. sankat maa paarnu

jerk / n. dhakka

jew / n. yahudi

jewel / n. ratna

job / n. kaam

join / v. jodnu; sangai basnu

joint / adj. samyukta; mileko

joke / n. thattaa

journal / n. patrikaa

journalism / n. patrakaaritaa

journalist / n. patrakaar

journey / n. yaatraa

joy / n. aananda; sukha

jubilee / n. utsab

judge / n. nyaayaadhish

judge / v. nirnaya garnu

judgement / n. aparaadh ko sajaay; phaisalaa

judiciary / adj. nyaayapaalikaa

juice / n. ras

juicy / adj. rasilo

jump / v. uphranu

jungle / n. forest

junior / n. kam umerko; tallo tahako
jurisdiction / n. adhikaar kshetra
just / adj. thik; uchit
just / adv. maatra
justice / n. nyaaya
justify / v. pramaanit garnu
juvenile / n. baalaparaadhi
keen / adj. utsuk
keep / v. raakhnu
kerosene / n. mattitel
key / n. saancho
kick / v. latti haannu
kid / n. bachchaa
kidnap / v. apaharan garnu
kidney / n. mirgaulaa
kidney bean / n. simi
kill / v. maarnu
kin / n. sambandhi
kind / adj. dayaalu
king / n. raajaa
kingdom / n. adhiraajya

kiss / v. chumban garnu; mwaai khaanu
kitchen / n. bhaansaa
kite / n. changaa
knee / n. ghundaa
knife / n. chakku
knit / v. bunnu
knock / v. khatkhat garnu
know / v. jaannu
knowledge / n. gyaan
labor / n. shram; mehanat
lack / n. kami
ladder /n. bhareng
lady / n. mahilaa
lake / n. taal; talaau
lame / adj. langado
lamp / n. batti
land / n. bhumi, jamin
landloard / n. ghardhani; jaggaadhani
landslide / n. pahiro
land-tax / n. maalpot
lane / n. galli

lantern / n. laaltin

lap / n. kaakh

large / adj. thulo

lash / n. korraa

last / n. antim adv. antamaa

lasting / adj. tikaau

late / adj. aber

lately / adv. haalai

later / adj. pachhi

latest / adj. sabhandaa nayaa

latrine / n. charpi

laugh / v. haasnu

laughter / n. haaso

laundry / n. lugaa dhune thaaun

law / n. kanoon

lawsuit / n. muddaa; naalish

lawyer / n. wakil

lay / v. paltanu

layman / n. saamanya byakti

lazy / adj. alchhi

lead / n. sisaa

lead / v. laijaanu; baato dekhaaunu

leader / n. netaa

leaf / n. paat

leak / v. chuhinu

lean / n. dublo

leaning / n. jhukaab

leap / v. uphranu

learn / v. siknu

learned / adj. bidwaan

lease / v. ghar bhaadaamaa dinu

least /n. kam se kam

leather / n. chhaalaa

leave / v. bidda

leave / v. chhodnu

lecture / n. bhaasan

lecturer / n. praadhyaapak

leech / n. jukaa

left / adj. baayaa

leg / n. khutta

legend / n. kathaa

legislature / n. bidhaan sabhaa

legitimate / adj. uchit

leisure / n. chhutti; abakaash

lemon / n. kaagati

lemon squash / n. kaagati ko sharbat

lend / v. saapat dinu

length / n. lambaai

lenient / adj. dayaalu

lentil / n. daal

leopard / n. chituwaa

less / adj. kam

less / adv. alikati

lessen / v. kam garnu

lesson / n. paath

letter / n. chitthi

level / n. samma

liability / n. uttardaayitwa; kharcha

libel / n. gaali; beijjati

liberal / n. udaar

liberate / v. mukta garnu

liberation / n. mukti

liberty / n. swatantrataa

library / n. pustakaalaya
lice / n. jumraa
license / n. anumati
lick / v. chaatun
lie / n. jhuto
lie / v. jhuto bolnu
lieu / n. satta
life / n. jiwan
lifelong / adj. baanchunjel; jiwan paryanta
lift / v. uthaaunu
light / adj. halkaa n. ujyaalo
lightning / n. bijuli
like / n. jasto
like / v. man paraaunu
likelihood / n. sambhaabanaa
likely / adj. sambhab
liking / n. man paraaunu; abhiruchi
limit / n. seemaa
limitation / n. pratibandha
limited / adj. seemit
line / n. rekhaa

lingua franca / n. rashtra bhashaa

link / v. jodnu

lion / n. singha

lip / n. oth

liquid / n. taral padaartha

liquor / n. raksi

list / n. naamaabali; suchana

listen / v. dhyaan diyera sunnu

literacy / n. saaksharataa

literature / n. saahitya

litter / v. phohor phaalnu

little / adj. alikati

live / v. baachnu

livestock / n. gaaibastu

living / n. jiwikaa

living / adj. jiwit

load / n. bhaari

loaf / n. paauroti

loan / n. rin; saapati

local / adj. sthaaniya

locate / v. pattaa lagaaunu

lock / talchaa
lock / v. talchaa marnu
lodge / n. asthhaayi basne thaaun
lodging / n. niwas; basne thaaun
log / adj. mudhaa
long / adj. laamo
look / v. hernu
loose / adj. phitalo
lord / n. prabhu; maalik
lose / v. haraaunu
loss / n.   . noksaan; naash
lost / adj. haraaeko
lotus / n. kamal
loud / n. thulo swarle
lousy / adj. kharaab; naraamro
love / n. prem
love / v. prem garnu
lovely / adj. sundar; raamro
lover / n. premi
loving / adj. priya; pyaaro
low / adj. tala; hocho

loyal / adj. bhakta

luck / n. bhaagya

lucky / adj. bhaagyamani

lucrative / adj. phaayada hune; laabhkar

luggage / n. maal saamaan

lumber / n. kaath

lunar / adj. chandramaa sambandhi

lunatic / n. baulaha; paagal

lure / v. lobhyaaunu

luxurious / adj. bilaasi; ati sukh

mandate / n. aadesh

mango / n. aanp

manipulate / v. chhal kapatle prabhandha garnu

mankind / n. maanab jaati

manner / n. kaam garne dhanga; tarika; shistaachaar

manpower / n. janashakti

manufacture / v. nirmaan garnu; banaaunu

manure / n. mal

manuscript / n. hastalikhit

many / adj. dherai

map / n. naksaa

marble / n. sangamarmar

margin / n. kinaara; chheu

mark / n. chino

market / n. bajaar

marketing / n. kinmel

marriage / n. bihaa; bihaah

marry / v. biha garnu

machine / n. mesin

mad / adj. bahulaa; paagal

magazine / n. patrikaa

magic / n. jaadu

magnet / n. chumbak

magnificent / adj. dherai raamro; sarbottam

mail / n. daak; hulaak

main / adj. mukhya

maize / n. makai

mainly / adv. mukhya ruple

maintain / v. sambhaar garnu

maintenance / n. sambhaar

majority / n. bahusamkhyak

make / v. banaaunu

malaria / n. aulo
male / n. purush; lognemanchhe
malice / n. irshyaa
man / n. maanis
manage / v. chalaaunu; bandobasta garnu
management / n. prabandha; bandobasta
manager / n. byabasthaapak; myanejar
martial / adj. senaa sambandhi; sainik
martyr / n. shaheed
marvellous / adj. aashcharya laagne
mask / n. mukundo
mason / n. dakarmi
mass / n. thupro
massage / n. maalish
massive / adj. thulo
master / n. maalik; shikshak
match / n. pratiyogitaa; samaan; salaai
mate / n. saathi
material / n. bastu
mathematics / n. ganit; hisaab
mattress /n chataai

mature / adj. praudh; paripakwa; paako
maximum / n. adhikatam; sabhandaa dherai
meadow / n. chaur
meal / n. khaanaa
mean / adj. neech; chhoto
meaning / n. maane
measles / n. daaduraa
measure / n. naap
measure / v. naapnu
measurement / n. naapi
meat / n. maasu
mechanic / n. mistri
medal / n. takmaa; padak
mediator / n. madhyastha
medical / adj. aushadhi baare
medicine / n. aushadhi
medieval / adj. madhya yug
meditation / n. dhyaan
medium / adj. maadhyam
meet / v. bhetnu
meeting / n. sabhaa; bhet

melt / v. paglanu
member / n. sadasya
memorial / n. smaarak
memory / n. samjhana
mental / adj. maanasik
mention / v. charchaa garnu; bhannu
menu / n. menyu; bhojaan ko suchi
mercenary / n. bideshmaa kaam garne sipaahi
merchant / n. saahu; mahaajan
merciful / adj. dayaalu
mercy / n. kripaa; dayaa
mere / adj. maatra
merge / v. ek hunu; milnu
merit / n. gun
merry / adj. prasanna; khushi
mess / n. gadbad
message / n. sandesh; samachaar
metal / n.dhaatu
method / n. tarkiaa
mid / adj. beech; madhya
middle / n. beechko bhaag; madhya bhaag

midnight / n. aadhaa rat; madhya raatri

might / n. bal

migrate / v. basaai saraai garnu

migration / n. basaai saraai

military / n. senaa

milk / n. dudh

million / n. das laakh

millionaire / n. lakhapati

mince / v. tukraa tukraa garnu

mind / n. man

mine / n. khaani

mineral / n. khanij padaartha

mingle / v. milnu; misinu

minimum / n. kam se kam

minister / n. mantri

ministry / n. mantraalaya

minor / n. naabaalak

minority / n. alpa sakhyak

ministrel / n. gaaine

minute / n. minet

miracle / n. chamatkar

mirror / n. ainaa

misbehaviour / n. ashista byabahaar

miscellaneous / adj. bibidh

mischief / n. upadrab

mischievous / adj. upadrabi

misdemeanour / n. saano aparaadh

miser / n. kanjoos

misfit / n. kaam na laggne

misfortunre / n. durbhaagya

mislead / v. dhokaa dinu

miss / n. kumari

miss / v. chuknu

missionary / n. dharma prachaarak

mistake / n. bhool

misunderstanding / n. galatphahami

mix / v. misinu

mixed / adj. mishrit; chhyaasmise

mob / n. bheed

modern / adj. aadhunik

modest / adj. saadhaaran; saumya

modify / v. badalnu

moment / n. chhin; kshyan

monarchy / n. adhiraajya

monastery / n. bihaar; math

monday / n. sombaar

money / n. paisaa; dhan

money order / n. dhanaadesh

monk / n. jogi; sanyaasi

monkey / n. baandar

monsoon / n. barkhaa

monster / n. raakshas

month / n. mahinaa

monthly / adj. prati mahinaa

moon / n. chandramaa

moonlight / n. jun

moral / adj. naitik

more / n. badhi; adhik

morning / n. bihaana

moslem / n. musalmaan

mosque / n. masjid

mosquito / n. laamkhutte

most / n. dherai

mother / n. aamaa

mother-in-law / n. saasu

mother-tongue / n. maatri bhaashaa

motive / n. uddeshya

mountain / n. pahaad

mountaineering / n. parbataarohan

mourn / v. dukha manaaunu

mouring / n. shok

mouse / n. musaa

mouth / n. mukh

move / v. chalnu; hatnu

movies / n. sinemaa

much / n. dherai

mud / n. hilo

mule / n. khachchad

multilateral / adj. bahu-pakshiya

multiply / v. gunaa garnu

mumps / n. haade

municipality / n. nagarpaalikaa

murder / n. hatyaa

murderer / n. hatyaaraa, jyaanmaaraa

music / n. sangeet; gaanaa
mutual / adj. aapasko
my / pron. mero
mystery / n. rahasya
myth / n. kalpanaako kathaa
nail / n. nang
name / n. naam
narrow / adj. saanguro
nation / n. raashtra
national / adj. raashtriya
natural / adj. swaabhaabik
nature / n. prakriti
near / adj. najik
nearly / adv. jhandai
neat / adj. saphaa
necessary / adj. aabashyak
neck / n. ghaanti
need / n. aabashyakata; chaahine
needle / n. siyo
neglect / v. bewaastaa garnu
neighbour / n. chhimeki

neighbourhood / n. chhimekmaa; waripari
neither / conj. na
nephew / n. bhatijaa
net / n. jaal
never / adv. kahile pani hoina
new / adj. nayaa
news / n. samaachaar; khabar
newspaper / n. samaachaar patra; akhbaar
next / adj. arko; tyaspacchhiko
nice / adj. raamro
nobody / n. kohipani hoina
noise / n. aabaaj; hallaa
none / pron. kohi pani hoina
noon / n. madhyaanaa
nor / conj. na
north / adv. uttar
northern / adj. uttari
nose / n. naak
not / adv. na
nothing / adv. kehi pani chhaina
now / adv. ahile

now a days / adv. aajkal

nowhere / adv. kahin pani hoina

nuclear / n. aanabik

nude / adj. naango

nuisance / n. baadhaa

number / n. nambar; sankhyaa

numerous / adj. anek

nut / n. supaari

nutrition / n. poshan

nutritious / adj. paushtik

oath / n. sapath

obedient / adj. aagyaakaari

obey / v. maannu

object / n. bastu; cheej; kuraa

objection / n. aapatti

objective / n. uddeshya

obscene / adj. ashleel

observation / n. abalokan

observe / v. manaaunu; hernu

obstacle / n. baadhaa

obstinate / adj. dhipi garne

obtain / v. paaunu
occasion / n. absar; maukaa
occasional / adj. kahile kaahi
occupation / n. peshaa
occupy / v. kabjaa garnu; basnu
ocean / n. samudra
odd / adj. anautho
odour / n. gandha
of / prep. ko
offer / n. prastaab
offer / v. dinu
office / n. aaphis; kaaryaalaya
officer / n. karmachaari
official / adj. sarkaari
often / adj. aksar
oil / adv. tel
ok / adv. theek
old / adj. budho; puraano
omit / v. na raakhnu; samaabesh nagarnu
on / prep. maa; maathi
once / adv. ekpalta

one / num ek

onion / n. pyaaj

only / adj. maatra

open / adj. khulaa

openly / adv. khulaa sita

operate / v. kaam garnu

operation / n. kaam; kaarbaahi

opinion / n. bhanaai; bichaar

opium / n. aphim

opponent / n. birodhi

opportunity / n. absar

oppose / v. birodh garnu

opposite / adj. biruddha; ulto

opposition / n. birodh; birodhi pakshya

oppress / v. dabaaunu

oppression / n. atyaachaar

or / conj. ya; athabaa

orange / n. suntalaa

order / n. aagya; byabasthaa

order / v. aagyaa dinu; magaaunu

ordinary / adj. saadhaaran; saamaanya

organization / n. samsthaa; sangathan

organize / v. byabasthaa garnu

original / adj. maulik

ornament / n. gahanaa

orthodox / adj. kattar

other / pron. aarko

otherwise / adv. anyathaa; natra

our / adj. haamro

out / adv. baahira

outcome / n. parinaam

outdoors / adj. ghar baahira

outside / n. baahir

outsider / n. baahiriyaa

over / prep. maathi; bhanda; badhi

owe / v. rin laageko hunu

own / adj. aaphno

own / v. aaphno hunu

owner / n. maalik; dhani

ox / n. saade

page / n. pannaa

pain / n. dukkha

painful / adj. dukhadaayi
painter /n. chitrakaar
painting / n. chitra
paper / n. kaagaj
paradise / n. swarga
parliament / n. sansad
pardon/ n. maaph
pardon / v. maaph garnu
parent / n. baabu aamaa
parrot / n. sugaa
part / n. bhaag
participate / v. bhaag linu
particular / adj. bishesh
partition / n. bibhaajan
party / n. dal
pass / v. uttirna hunu; pass hunu
passage / n. baato
passanger / n. yaatri
passport / n. raahadaani
past / adj. biteko
path / n. baato; sadak

patience / n. dhairya
patient / n. rogi; biraami
patriotic / adj. desh bhakta
pay / v. tirnu
pay / n. talab
peace / n. shaanti
penalty / n. danda; sajaaya
pencil / n. sisaa kalam
penetrate / v. ghusnu; pasnu
people / n. maanis; janataa
pepper / n. khursaani
perfect / adj. bilkul theek; purna
perform / v. kaam garnu
performance / n. kaam garaai;
perfume / n. sugandha; baasnaa
perhaps / adv. shaayad
period / n. abadhi
permanent / n. sthaayi
permit / n. anumati
person / n. byakti
personal / adj. byaktigat

personally / adv. byaktigat ruple
persuade / v. manaaunu
philosophy / n. darshan
photo / n. photo; tasbeer
physician / n. daaktar
piece / n. tukraa
pig / n. sungur
pigeon / n. parewaa
pilgrim / n. tirthayaatri
pillow / n. takiyaa
pity / n. dukha ko kuraa
place / n. thaaun
place / v. raakhnu
plain / adj. saadaa
plain / n., maidaan
plane / n. hawaaijahaaj
planet / n. graha
plant / n biruwaa
play / n. khel; v. khelnu
player / n. khelaadi
pleasant / n. raamro

please / v. kripayaa
pleasure / n. aananda
plenty / n. prasasta
plot / n. shadyantra
plum / n. aalubakhadaa
pocket / n. jeb; paaket; khalti
poet / n. kabi
poetry / n. kabitaa
point / n. bindu; mukhya kuraa
point / v. dekhaaunu
poison / n. bikh
police / n. pulis; prahari
policy / n. niti
polite / adj. namra
political / adj. raajnaitik
politics / n. raajniti
poor / adj. gareeb
popular / adj. lokapriya
popularity / n. lokapriyataa
population / n. janasnkhyaa
position / n. thaaun; darjaa

possession / n. dhan sampatti; bhog chalan
possibility / n. sambhaabana
possible / adj. sambhab
post / n. daak; v. pathaaunu
post office / n. daak ghar
postpone / n. sthagit garnu
pot / n. bhaado
poverty / n. garibi
powder / n. dhulo
power / n. shakti
powerful / adj. shaktishaali
practical / adj. byaabahaarik
practice / n. abhyaas
practice / v. abhyaas garnu
praise / n. prashamshaa
praise / v. prashamshaa garnu
pray / v. praarthanaa garnu
prayer / n. praarthanaa
preach / v. dharma prachaar garnu
precious / adj. bahumulya
prefer / v. badhataa ruchaaunu

pregnant / adj. garbhini; pet bokeko
prejudice / n. purbadhaaranaa
preparation / n. tayaari
prepare / v. tayaar garnu
present / adj. haajiri
present / n. haajir
preserve / v. rakshaa garnu
president / n. raashtrapati
press / v. dabaaunu
prestige / n. ijjat; sanmaan
pretend / v. bahaanaa garnu
pretty / adj. raamro
prevent / v. roknu
previous / adj. pahileko
price / n. mol
pride / n. garba
priest / n. purohit
primary / adj. praathamik
print / v. chhaapnu
prison / n. jel; kaid
prisoner / n. kaidi; bandi

private / adj. niji; byaktigat

prize / n. inaam; purashkaar

probably / adv. hola; shaayad

probability / n. sambhaabana; hola jasto

problem / n. samasyaa

procession / n. julus

produce / v. utpaadan garnu

profession / n. peshaa

professor / n. praadhyaapak; profesar

profit / n. naaphaa

progress / n. kaaryakaram

progress / n. unnati

promise / n. pratigyaa

pronounce / v. uchchaaran garnu

proof / n. pramaan

proper / adj. uchit

properly / adv. uchit kisim baata

property / n. sampatti

proposal / n. prastaab

prostitute / n. randi; beshyaa

protect / v. rakshaa garnu; bachaaunu

protection / n. rakshaa
prove / v. siddha garnu
provide / v. dinu; byabasthaa garnu
provisional / adj. asthaayi
public / n. janataa
public / adj. saarbajanik
pull / v. taannu
punish / v. sajaaya dinu
punishment / n. sajaaya
pupil / n. bidyaarthi
purchase / v. kinmel garnu
pure / adj. shuddha
purpose / n. uddeshya
push / v. dhakelnu
put / v. raakhnu
qualification / n. yogyataa
qualified / adj. yogya; laayak
quarrel / n. jhagadaa
quarter / n. ek chauthaai
queen / n. raani
question / n. prashna; sawaal

quick / adj. chhito
quiet / adj. shaanta
quilt / n. sirag
quit / v. chhodnu
quite / adv. ekdam; puraa tawarle
race / n. jaati
radio / n. redio
raddish / n. gaajar
raid / n. hamalaa
raid / n. hamalaa garnu
rail / n. rel
rain / n. barsaa; paani
rain / v. paani parnu
rainbow / n. indradhanush
raise / v. uthaaunu
raisin / n. daakh; kismis
rank / n. darjaa
rape / n. balaatkaar
rare / adj. durlabh
rarely / adv. biralai; kahilekaahi
rat / n. muso

rate / n. dar
ratio / n. anupaat
raw / n. kaacho
reach / v. pugnu
read / v. padhnu
ready / adj. tayaar
real / adj. baastabik
reality / n. basstabiktaa
really / adj. baastabmaa
realistic / adj. byaabahaarik
realize / v. thaahaa paaunu; bujhnu
reason / n. kaaran
rebel / n. birodhi
rebellion / n. bidroha
recall / v. samjhanu
receipt / n. rasid
receive / v. paaunu
recent / adj. haalaiko
recently / adv. haalsaalai
reception / n. swaagat samaaroh
reckless / adj. jathaabhaabi

recognize / v. chinnu; maanyataa dinu

recollect / v. samjhanu

recollection / n. samjhanaa

recommend / v. sifaarish garnu

recommendation / n. sifaarish

recover / v. pheri paaunu; bisek hunu

recruit / v. bharnaa garnu

recruitment / n. bharnaa

rectify / v. sudhaar garnu

rectum / n. chaak

red / adj. raato

reduce / v. ghataaunu

reduction / n. ghatnu

redundant / adj. anaabashyak

refer / v. ullekh garnu

reference / n. prasanga; ullek

reform /v. sudhaar garnu

reform / n. sudhaar

reformer / n. sudhaarak

refreshment / n. chiyaa paani; chamenaa

refugee / n. sharanaarthi

refund /v. paisaapharkaaunu

refusal / n. aswikriti

refuse / v. asweekaar garnu

regard / v. mannu

regard / n. aadar

regarding / adj. baaremaa

regardless / adv. hundaahundaipani

regret / n. dukha; khed

regret / v. khed garnu

regular / adj. niyamit

regularly / adv. niyamit ruple

rejoice / v. khushi hunu

related / adj. sambhandit

relation / n. sambandhi; naataaparne

relax / v. aaraam garnu

relay / v. prasaar garnu

release / v. chhodi dinu

religion / n. dharma

religious / adj. dhaarmik

reluctant / adj. man naparaune

remain / v. rahanu

remark / n. bhanaai
remakrable / adj. mahatwapurna
remedy / n. aushadhi
remember / v. samjhanu
remind / v. samjhaaunu
remorse / n. pachhuto; paschaattap
remote / adj. durgam; taadhaako
remove / v. hataaunu
rent / n. bhaadaa; kiraayaa
rent / v. bhaadaamaa dinu
repair / v. marammat garnu
repatriation / n. ghar pharkanu
reply / v. jabab dinu
reply / n. uttar; jabaab
report / n. pratibedan
represent / v. pratinidhitwa garnu
representative / n. pratinidhi
reprimand / n. chetaawani
republic / n. ganaraajya
reputation / n. ijjat
request / v. anurodh garnu

request / n. anurodh
requirement / n. aabashyakataa
rescue / v. bachaaunu
rescue / n. bachaawat
research / n. anusandhaan
resemble / v. jasto dekhinu
reserve / v. jagedaa raakhnu
reservoir / n. jalaashaya
reside / v. basnu; niwass garnu
residence / n. niwas
resident / n. niwas
resign / v. raajinaamaa garnu; tyaagpatra dinu
resist / v. birodh garnu
resistance / n. birodh
respect / n. aadar
respect / v. aadar garnu
respectable / adj. aadaraniya
responsibility / n. uttardaayitwa
responsible / adj. uttardaayi
rest / n. aaraam; bishraam
rest / v. aaraam garnu

restaurant / n. resturant
restroom / n. baathrum
result / n. parinaam
retaliate / v. jabaabi hamalaa garnu
retire / v. abakaash linu
retirement / n. abakaash
return / v. pharkanu
reunion / n. punarmilan
reveal / v. rahasya kholnu
revenge / n. badalaa
reverse / v. ultaaunu
reward / n. purashkaar; inaam
review / v. punarabalokan garnu
revolution / n. kraanti
revolutionary / adj. kraantikaari
rhodendrodron / n. guraans
rice / n. bhaat; chaamal
rich / adj. dhani
riches / n. dhan daulat
ride / v. chadhnu
right / adj. theek; daahine

right / n. adhikar

ring / n. bajnu

ring / n. aunthi

riot / n. dangaa

ripe / adj. paakeko

rise / v. uthnu

rising / n. utheko; udaaeko

risk / n. khataraa; dar

ritual / n. dhaarmik; kriyaa

rival / n. pratidwandi

river / n. nadi

road / n. sadak

roam / v. ghumnu

roar / v. garjanu

roast / v. seknu

rob / v. daakaa daalnu

robber / n. daaku

rock / n. chattaan

roll / v. berinu

romance / n. premaalaap

roof / n. chhaanaa

room / n. kothaa
root / n. jaraa
rope / n. dori
rose / n. gulaaf
rot / v. sadnu
rotate / v. ghumnu
rotation / n. ghumaai
rotten / adj. kuheko
rough / adj. khasro
route / n. baato
routine / n. dainik kaam, niyamit kaam
royal / adj. raajakiya; shaahi
royal army / shaahi senaa
royalist / n. raajbhakta; raajaamaanne
rub / v. dalnu
rubber / n. rabar
rude / adj. besomati; rukhi
rug / n. kambal; paakhi
ruin / n. khandahaar
ruin / v. barbaad garnu
rule / n. shaasan; niyam

rule / v. raajya garnu
ruler / n. shashak
rumor / n. halla
run / v. dagurnu
runaway / n. bhaageko
rupee / n. rupaiyaa
rural / adj. grameen
rush / n. hatpat; hataar
rush / v. chaadai jaanu
rust / n. khiyaa
ruthless / n. nirdayi
sabotage / n. bigaar
sack / n. boraa
sack / v. barkhaasta garnu
sacred / adj. pabitra
sacrifice / n. balidaan
sad / adj. dukhi; dikdaar
saddle / n. kaathi
safe / n. surakshit; dar nalaagne
safety / n. surakshaa
saffron / n. keshar

sailor / n. maajhi

salary / n. talab

sale / n. bikri

salesman / n. bikretaa; pasale

salient / adj. mukhya

salt / n. noon

salty / adj. nunilo

salute / adj. abhibaadan garnu

salvation / n. mukti

same / adj. uhi

sample / n. namoonaa

sand / n. baluwaa

sandle / n. chappal

sapphire / n. nilam

sanitary / n. saphaa sughhar

sanitation / n. saphaai; swachchhataa

satellite / n. upagraha

satire / n. byanga

satisfaction / n. santosh

satisfactory / adj. santoshprad

satisfy / v. santosh garnu

saturday / n. sanibaar
saucer / n. rikaapi
savage / n. jangali
save / v. bachaaunu
saw / n. karaunti
say / v. bhannu
saying / n. bhanaai
scale / n. naap
scar / n. daag
scarce / adj. kam; abhaab
scarcely / adv. muskille
scarf / n. galbandi
scatter / v. chharnu
scene / n. drishya; ghatanaa sthal
schedule / n. samaya taalikaa
scheme / n. aayojanaa
scholar / n. bidwaan
school / n. skul; bidyaalaya
science / n. bigyaan
scientific / adj. baigyaanik
scientist / n. baigyaanik

scissor / n. kainchi

scratch / n.saano ghaau

scream / v. chichyaaunu

sea / n. samudra

search / v. khojnu

search / n. khoji

season / nn. mausam

seat / n. basne thaaun; sthaan

secede / v. chhuttinu

second / adj. dosro

secret / adj. gopya

secretary / n. sachib

secretariat / n. sachibaalaya

sector / n. khanda

secular / n. dharma nirapekshya

secure / adj. surakshit

security / n. surakshyaa

sedition / n. raajadroha

seduce / v. phakaaunu

see / v. hernu

see off / v. bidaa garnu

seed / n. biu
seek / n. khojnu
select / v. chhannu
selection / n. chhanaawat
seize / v. samaatnu; hatyaaunu
seldom / adv. kahile kaahi
self / pron. aaphu
selfish / adj. swaarthi
sell / v. bechnu
seller / n. bikretaa
seminar / n. goshti
send / v. pathaaunu
senior / adj. jetho; barishta
sense / n. hosh
senseless / adj. behosh
senstitive / adj. sambedanshil
sentence / n. baakya; phaisalaa
separate / adj. beglai
separate / v. chhutyaaunu
separation / n. bibhaajan
serious / adj. gambhir

servant / n. nokar; sewak
serve / v. sewaa garnu
service / n. sewaa; nokari
session /n. baithak
set / n. samuha
settle / v. milaaunu; basobaas garnu
settlement / n. basti
several / adj. dherai
severe / adj. kadaa
sew / v. siunu
sex / n. yaun
shadow / n. chhayaa
shadow / v. pachhi laagnu
shake / v. hallaaunu, milaaunu
shallow / n. kam gahiro
shame / n. laaj
shape / v. roop dinu
shape / n. aakaar; roop
share / n. amsha; bhaag
share / v. bhaag lagaaunu
sharp / adj. teekho

shave / v. daadhi kaatnu
she / pron. uni; u
sheep / n. bhedaa
shelf / n. daraaj
shelter / n. aashraya
shepherd / n. gothaalo
sherpa / n. tribal group living in Everest area
shift / v. sarnu
shine / v. chamkanu
ship / n. jahaaj
shirt / n. kamij
shock / n. dhakka
shoe / n. juttaa
shoot / v. haannu (bandukle)
shop / n. pasal
shop / v. kinmel garnu
shore / n. kinaaraa
short / adv. chhoto
shortage / n. kami
shortly / adv. chaadai
shoulder / n. kaandh

shout / v. karaaunu; chichyaaunu
show / v. dekhaaunu
shower / n. snaan
shut / v. banda garnu
shy / adj. laaj maanne
sick / adj. biraami
side / n. chheu
sidewalk / n. sadakko peti
sight / v. drishya
sign / v. sahi garnu
signature / n. sahichhap
signal / n. ishaaraa
silence / n. chupki; maunataa
silk / n. resham
silver / n. chaadi
sin / n. paap
since / adv. tyaspachhi
sincere / adv. sachcha
sing / v. gaaunu
single / adj. eklo; abibaahit
sink / v. dubnu

sir / n. mahaashaya; saaheb
sister / n. bahini; didi
sit / v. basnu
situation / n. sthiti
six / adj. chha
skeleton / n. kankaal
skill / n. dakshataa
skillful / n. dakshya
skin / n. chhaalaa
sky / n. aakaash
slave / n. kamaaro; daas
slavery / n. daasataa
sleep / n. nidraa
sleep / v. nidaaunu
slay / n. maarnu
slight / adj. alikati
slim / adj. dublo; paatalo
slip / v. chiplanu
slow / adj. jumso
slowly / adv. bistaarai
small / adj. saano

smallpox / n. biphar
smart / adj. chharito; phurtilo
smell / v. gandha aaunu
smell / n. baasna; gandha
smile / v. muskuraaunu
smile / n. muskaan
smoke / v. churot khaanu; dhumrapaan garnu
smoke / n. dhuwaa
smoker / n. churot khaane byakti
smooth / adj. eknaasko, chiplo
snake / n. sarpa
sneeze / v. chhiun garnu
snore / v. ghurnu
snow / n. hiun; baraph
snow / v. hinu parnu
so / adv. yasaile
so called / adj. tathaa kathit
soak / v. bhijnu
soap / n. saabun
social / adj. saamaajik
socialism / samaajbaad

socialize / v. milansaar hunu
society / n. samaaj
sociology / n. samaajshastra
sock / n. mojaa
soft / adj. naram
soften / naram parnu
soil / n. maato
solar / adj. surya sambandhi
soldier / n. sipaahi
solely / adv. kebal; ekmaatra
solid / adj. thos
solidarity / nn. ektaabhaab
solution / n. samaadhaan; jhol
solve / v. samaadhan garnu
some / adj. kehi
somebody / pron. kunai byakti
somehow / adv. kunai prakaarle
something / n. kunai kuraa
sometimes / n. kunaibelaa; kahilekaahin
somewhat / adv. kehiroopmaa
somewhere / adv. kunai thaaunmaa

son / n. chhoraa

song / n. gaanaa

son-in-law / jwaai

soon / adv. chaadai

sophisticated / adj. parishkrit

sorrow / n. aatmaa

soul / n. aatmaa

sound / n. aawaaj

sound / adj. gatilo

sour / adj. amilo

source / n. shrot

south / adj. dakshin

southern / adj. dakshini

souvenir / n. chino

soverign / adj. saarbabhaum

sow / v. ropnu

soyabean / n. bhatmaas

space / n. antariksha

space / v. thaaun milaaunu

spare / v. baanki raakhnu

spare / n. baanki

spark / n. jhilkaa

sparrow / n. bhangeraa

speak / v. bolnu

speaker / n. baktaa

special / adj. bishesh

specialist / n. bishesagya

specially / adv. bishesh gari

specify / v. toknu

spectacles / n. chasmaa

speech / n. bhaasha

speed / n. gati; beg

speed / v. kudaaunu

spell / n. tunaa; mohini

spend / v. bitaaunu (time), kharcha garnu (money)

spit / v. thuknu

splendid / adj. shaandaar

split / v. chhuttinu

spoil / v. bigaarnu

sport / n. khel

spouse / n. logne; swaasni

spread / v. phailanu

spring / adj. basanta
spring / v. uphrinu
staff / n. karmachaari
stain / n. dhabba; daag
stain / v. daag laagnu
stair / n. bhareng
stamp / tikat; chhap
stamp / v. chhaap lagaaunu
stand / v. ubhinu
standard / n. stariya
star / n. taaraa; kalaakaar
start / n. shuru
start / v. shuru garnu
state / v. raajya; awasthaa
state / v. bhannu
statement / n. bhanaai; baktabya
station / n. steshan
statue / n. mutri; ain
status / n. pad
stay / v. basnu
stay / n. basaai

steady / adj. lagaataar

steal / v. chornu

steam / n. baraph

steep / adj. bhiraalo; ukaalo

step / n. paailaa

stick / n. lathi

stick / v. taasinu

stiff / adj. kadaa

still / adj. shaanta

still / adv. taipani

stir / v. chalaaunu

stock / v. bechne maalsaamaan

stomach / n. pet

stone / n. dhungaa

stop / v. roknu

stop / n. roktok

store / n. godaam

store / v. jammaa gari raakhnu

storm / n. aandhi

story / n. kathaa

stout / adj. moto

straight / adj. seedhaa; sojho
strange / adj. bichitrako
stranger / n. aparichit
straw / n. khar; paraal
stream / n. kholaa
street / n. sadak
strength / n. bal
strict / adj. kadaa; sakhta
strike / v. haannu
strike / n. hartaal
string / n. dhaago; dori
stroll / n. ghumaai
stroll / v. ghumnu
strong / adj. baliyo
struggle / n. sangharsha
struggle / v. ladnu
study / n. adhyayan
study / v. adhyayan garnu
stuff / n. chijbij
stupid / adj. murkha
subject / n. bishaya; prajaa

submission / n. samarpan
subside / v. ghatnu
substance / n. saaraansh
succeed / v. saphal hunu
success / n. saphalataa
successful / adj. saphal
such / adj. yasto
suddenly / adv. ekaaek; akasmaat
suffer / v. dukha paaunu
sugar / n. chini
suggest / v. sujhaab dinu
suggestion / n. sujhaab
suicide / n. aatmahatyaa
suit / v. suhaaundo hunu
suit / n. mudda; naalish
summary / n. saaraamsha
summer / n. garmi
summit / n. shikhar; taakuro
sun / n. ghaam; surya
sunday / n. aaitabaar
sunny / adj. ghaam laageko

sunshine / n. ghaam
supper / n. belukaako khaanaa
supply / v. jutaaunu
support / n. samarthan
suppose / v. anumaan garnu
supermacy / n. aadhipatya
sure /adj. pakkaa; nischaya
surface / n. sataha
surname / n. thar
surprise / n. aashcharya
surrender / n. aatmasamarpan
surrender / v. aatmasamarpan garnu
surround / v. ghernu
surroundings / n. waripari
suspicion / n. shankaa
swallow / v. khaanu; nilnu
swear / v. kiriyaa haalnu
sweat / n. pasinaa
sweat /v. pasinaa aaunu
sweet / adj. mitho
swell / v. sunninu

swim / v. paudanu; paudi khelnu
swim / n. paudi
swing / v. hallanu
sword / n. tarbaar
symbol / n. chino
sympathy / n. sahaanubhuti
syphat ize / v. sahaanubhuti dekhaaunu
system / n. byabasthaa; pranaali; riti
table / n. tebil
tact / n. dhanga
tail / n. puchchhar
tail / v. pachhi laagnu
tailor / n. sujikaar
take / v. linu; samaatnu
take away / v. laijaanu
take off / v. phukaalnu; udnu
take over /v adhikaarmaa linu
tale / n. kathaa
talent / n. pratibhaa
talk / n. kura
talk / v. kura garnu

talkative / adj. kuraaute; phatphate
tall / adj. alko
tame / v. paalnu
tame / n. ratieko
tank / n. tyaanki
tap / n. dhaaraa
taste / n. swaad
tasty / adj. swaadista
tax / n. kar
tax / v. kar lagaaunu
taxi / tyaksi
tea / n. chiyaa
teach / v. padhaaunu
teacher / n. sikshak; guru
tear / n. aansu
tear / v. chyaatnu
tease / v. jiskaaunu
technical / adj. praabidhik
telegraph / n. telegraph
telephone / n. telephon
television / n. telibisan

tell / v. bhannu
temper / n. ris
temperature / n. taapakram
temple / n. mandir
temproary / adj. asthaayi
tempt / v. lobhyaaunu
temptation / n. lobh; pralobhan
ten / n. das
tenant / n. mohi; bhaadaamaa basne
tend / v. jhuknu
tendency / n. jhukaab; prabritti
tension / n. tanaab
tent / n. paal
term / n. awadhi
terminate / v. tunginu
termite / n. dhamiro
terrible / adj. bhayankar
territory / n. kshetra
terror / n. aatanka
terrorist / adj. aatankabaadi
test / n. jaanch; parikshya

textbook / n. paathyapustak
than / conj. bhandaa
thank / v. dhanyabaad dinu
thank you / dhanyabaad
that / adj/ tyo; tyahi
theirs / pron. tiniharuko
then / adv. taba; tyaspachhi
these / adv. yi
therefore / adv. tyaskaaran; tyasaile
they / pl. pron. tiniharu; wahaaharu
thick / adj. baaklo; gaadhaa
thickness / n. baaklaai
theif / n. chor
thin / adj. paatalo
thing / n. chij; bastu
think / v. sochnu; bichaar garnu
third / adj. tesro
thirst / n. pyaas; tirkhaa
thirsty / adj. pyaaso; tirkhaaeko
this / adj. yo
through / adj. puraa; sampurna

thoroughly / adv. puraasita
thought / n. bichaar
thoughtful / adj. bichaarshil
thread / n. dhaago
threat / n. dhamki
threaten / v. dhamki dinu
throat / n. ghaanti
through / prep. dwaaraa; bhaera
throw / v. phyaaknu; phaalnu
thumb / n. budhi aunlaa
thunder / n. bajra
thus / adv. yasari; tyasari
ticket / n. tikat
tidy / adj. saphaa
tiger / n. baagh
tight / adj. kasieko
tighten / v. kasnu
till / prep. samma
till / v. jotnu
tiller / n. jotaahaa
timber / n. kaath; lakadi

time / n. samaya; belaa
timely / adv. maukaako
timetable / n. samaya taalikaa
timid / adj. lajaalu; laajmaanne
tip / n. bakas; bakhsheesh
tip / v. bakas dinu
tire / v. thaaknu
tired / adj. thaakeko
to / prep. laai; samma
tobacco / n. tamaakhu
today / adv. aaja
toe / n. khutta ko aunlaa
together / adv. sangai
tomorrow / adv. bholi
tongue / n. jibro; bhaasaa
tonight / n. aaja raati
too / adv. ati
too / conj. pani
tool / n. hatiyaar
tooth / n. daant
toothache / n. daantdukhne

top / n. tuppo; chuchuro
topic / n. bishaya
torture / n. yaatanaa
total / adj. jammaa; puraa
touch / n. samparka; sparsha
touch / v. chhunu
tough / v. kadaa
tour / n. bhraman
tour / v. ghumnu
tourist / n. paryatak
towards / prep. tira
towel / n. tauliyaa
tower / n. aglo bhawan; minaar
town / n. nagar; shahar
toy / n. khelaunaa
track / n. godeto
trade / n. byaapaar
trade / v. byaapaar garnu
trader / n. byaapaari
tradition / n. chalan
traditional / adj. chalan chaltiko

traffic / n. traphik
trail / n. baato; godeto
train / n. relgaadi
traitor / n. deshdrohi; gaddaar
translate / v. anubaad garnu
translation / n. anubaad
trap / n. khor
trap / v. khor thaapnu
travel / v. bhraman garnu
travel / n. bhraman
tray / n. kisti
treachery / n. biswaasghaat
treason / n. deshdroh
treasure / n. dhan
treasury / n kosh; dhukuti
treat / n. satkaar
treat / v. byabahaar garnu
tree / n. rukh; bot
trek / n. paidal ghumnu
trek / n. paidal ghumaai
tremble / v. kaapnu

trial / n. kaanuni purpakshya
tribal / adj. janajaatiya
tribe / n. janajati
tributary / n. shaakhaa
trick / v. jhukyaaunu
trick / n. chhal; kapat
trip / n. yaatraa
triumph / n. bijaya; jeet
troop / n. senaa; phauj
trouble / n. dukha; jhanjhat
trouser / n. suruwaal
true / adj. satya; saancho
truly / adv. saachai
trunk / n. rukh ko phed
trust / n. biswaas
trust / v. biswaas garnu
truth / n. saancho; satya
truthful / adj. satyabaadi
try / v. koshis garnu
tuesday / n. mangalbaar
tuition / n. phis; padhaaiko shulka

tune / n. swar; raag
tunnel / n. surung
turn / n. paalo
turn / v. pharkaaunu; ghumnu
turn back / v. pharkanu
turn off / v. banda garnu
turn on / v. kholnu
tutor / n. sikshak
twenty / adj. bees
twice / adv. dui palta
twin / adj. jumlyaahaa
two / num. dui
type / n. kisim
type / v. taip garnu
typical / adj. namunaa hune
tyre / n. tayar
tyranny / n. atyaachaar
tyrant / n. atyaachaari
ugly / adj. naraamro
ultimate / adj. aakhiri
ultimately / adv. aakhirmaa

umbrella / n. chhataa
unable / adj. asamartha
unacceptable / adj. asweekarya
unacquainted / adj. aparichit
unanimous / adj. ekmat
unarmed / adj. hatiyaar nabhaeko
unavoidable / adj. nabhai na hune
uncertain / adj. anischit
uncle / n. kakaa; kanchhaabaa
uncomfortable / adj. asubidhaajanak
unconscious / adj. behosh
undecided / adj. anischit
under / prep. tala
underground / jameen muniko
underneath / post prep. talatira
understand / v. bujhnu
understandable / adj. bujhna sakine
undertake / v. kaam garne
undesirable / adj. abaanchhaniya
unemployed / adj. bekaar
unemployment / adj. bekaari

uneasy / adj. asajilo; bechain
uneducated / adj. ashikshit
unequal / adj. asamaan
unexpected / adj. nachitaaeko
unfair / adj. anuchit
unforeseen / adj. pahile bichaar   gareko
unfortunate / adj. abhaagi
unfortunately / adj. durbhaagyabash
unhappy / adj. dukhi
unhealthy / adj. aswaasthakar
unheard / adj. nasunikeo
uniform / n. poshaak
uniform / adv. eknaas
unification / n. ekikaran
unify / v. ek parnu; ekikaran garnu
unilateral / adj. ekpaskshiya
union / n. sangha; ekikaran
unimportant / adj. mahatwahin
unit / n. ekaai
unite / v. ek paarnu
united / adj. samyukta

united states / samyukta raajya
united nations / samyukta raashtra
unity / n. ekataa
vacancy / n. khaali thaaun
vacant / adj. khaali
vacate / v. khaali garnu
vacation / n. bidaa; chhutti
vaccination / n. khopaai
vaccinate / v. khopnu
vague / adj. aspastha
vain / adj. sittaimaa
valid / adj. maanya
valley / n. upatyakaa; khaaldo
valuable / adj. bahumulya
value / n. mulya; mol
value / v. mahatwa dinu
vanish / v. haraaunu
vanity / n. ghamanda
vapour / n. baaph
variety / n. bibhinna; kisim
various / adj. kisim kisimko

vary / v. pharak hunu

vast / adj. bishaal; thulo

vegetable / n. tarkaari; saagpaat

vegetarian / n. shaakaahaari

vehicle / n. gaadi; sawaari

veil / n. pardaa; ghumto

vendor / n. bechne manchhe

veneral / adj. yaun sambandhi

vengeance / n. badalaa

universal / adj. bishwabyaapi

universe / n. bishwa; samsaar; brahmaanda

university / n. bishwabidyaalaya

unjust / adj. anuchit

unless / conj. natra

unlikely / adj. hunu gaaro

u paid / adj. natireko

unpleasant / adj. naramaailo

unreliable / adj. abishwasaniya

unrest / adj. bechain; shaanta na bhaeko

unsatisfactory / adj. asantoshprad

until / prep. conj. samma

unwilling / adj. anikshuk
up / adv. maathi
upper / adv. maathillo
uprising / n. birodh
upset / v. chintit
upstairs / adv. bhareng maathi
urban / adj. shahari
urge / v. garna lagaaunu
urgent / adj. ati jaroori
urine / n. pisaab
use / v. upayog garnu
use / n. upayog
verb / n. kriyaa
verbal / adj. maukhik
verge / n. chheu
verfication / n. jaanch
verify / v. jaanchnu
verse / n. shlok
vertical adj. thaado
very / adj. dherai
vessel / n. jahaaj; bhaado

viable / n. byaabahaarik
vice President / upa-rashtrapati
vicinity / n. chhimek
victim / n. pidit
victor / n. bijetaa
victorious / adj. bijayee
victory / n. bijaya; jeet
view / v. hernu
view / v. hernu
village / n. gaaun
villager / n. gaaunle
villain / n. kharaab manchhe
violence / n. himsaa
violent / adj. himsak
virtue / n. gun
visible / adj. dekhine
visibility / n. dekhine
visit / v. bhetnu
visit / n. bhet
visitor / n. aagantuk
vital / adj. mukhya; atyaabashyak

vocabulary / n. shabda bhandaar

voice / n. swar

void / n. shunya

volatile / adj. asthir

volcano / n. jwaalaamukhi

volume / n. aayatan

voluntary / adj. swechchhale

volunteer / n. swayamsewak

vomit / v. bantaa garnu

vote / v. matdaan garnu

vote / n. vot

vow / n. pratigyaa

vow / v. pratigyaa garnu

voyage / n. laamo yatraa; samudra yatraa

vulgar / adj. ashleel

vulnerable / adj. asurakshit

vulture / n. giddha

useful / adj. upayogi

useless / adj. kaam nalaagne

usual / adj. sadhai ko jasto

utensil / n. bhaadaa kudaa

utilize / v. kaam ma lyaaunu
wage / n. jyaalaa; paarishramik
wail / v. runu
waist / n. kammar
wait / v. parkhanu
waiting room / n. pratikshaalaya
waitor / n. beraa
wake / v. jaagnu; uthnu
wake up / v. biunjhaaunu
walk / v. hindnu
wall / n. parkhaal
wander / v. ghumphir garnu
want / v. chaahinu
war / n. ladaai
warehouse / n. godaam
warm / adj. nyaano
warmth / n. nyaanopan
warning / n. chetaawani
warrior / n. ladaaku; yoddhaa
wash / v. dhunu
washerman / n. dhobi

waste / v. barbaad garnu

waste / n. barbaadi

watch / v. hernu

watch / n. ghadi

watchful / adj. satarka

watchman / n. chaukidaar

water / n. paani

watermellon / n. tarbujaa

welcome / n. swaagat

welcome / v. swaagat garnu

well / adj. swastha

well / n. inaar

well / adv. raamrosita

well being / n. bhalo

well wisher / n. bhalo chaahane

west/ n. paschim

western / adj. paschimi

westward / adj. paschimitira

wet / adj. bhijeko

what / adj. ke

whatever / adj. jesukai

wheat / n. gahun
wheel / n. paangraa
when / adv. kahile
whenever / adv. junsukai belaamaa
where / adv. kahan; jahan
wherever / adv. junsukai thaaumaa
whether / conj. ya
which / pron. junsukai; kun
while / n. jahasamma
while / conj. jaba
whip / n. korraa
whisper / n. kaanekhushi
whisper / v. kaanekhushi garnu
whistle / n. suselo
white / adj. seto
who / pron. ko
whoever /pon. josukai
whole / adj. puraa; sampurna
wholesale / n. thok
wholesome / adj. hitkaari
whore / n. randi; beshyaa

why / adv. kina

wicked / adj. dusta

wide / adj. chaudaa; pharaakilo

widespread / adj. byaapak

widow / n. bidhwaa

width / n. chaudaai

wife / n. swaasni; patni; shrimati

wild / adj. jangali

will / n. ichchha; ichchhaapatra

will / v. ichchhaa garnu

win / v. jitnu

wind / n. haawaa

window / n. jhyaal

wing / n. pakhetaa

wind / n. haawaa

window / n. jhyaal

wine / n. rakshi

winner / n. bijetaa

winter / n. jaado

wipe / v. puchhnu

wire / n. taar

wisdom / n. buddhi

wise / n. buddhimaan

wish / v. chaahanu

witch / n. boksi

with / adv. bhitra; saath; sangai

without / adv. binaa

witness / n. saakshi

wolf / n. bwaaso

woman / n. aaimaai

wonder / n. aashcharya

wood / n. kaath

wool / n. un

word / n. shabda

work / v. kaam garnu

work / n. kaam

worker / n. majdur

world / n. samsaar

worm / n. kiraa

worried / adj. chintit

worry / n. chintaa garnu

worse / adj. kharaab

worsen / v. jhan kharaab hunu

worship / v. pujaa garnu

worship / n. pujaa

worthless / adj. kaam nalaagne

wound / n. ghaau

wrap / v. baandhnu

wrestling / n. kushti

wrinkle / n. chaauri

wrist / n. naari

write / v. lekhnu

writer / n. lekhak

wrong / adj. galat; betheek

yak / n. chaunri gaai

yard / n. gaj

year / n. barsa

yearly / adv. prati barsa

yell / v. chichyaaunu

yellow / n. pahelo

yes / n. ho; chha

yesterday / adv. hijo

yet / conj. ajha

yield / n. utpatti

yogurt / n. dahi

you / pron. timi; tapaai

your / adj. tapaaiko; timro

zeal / n. josh; utsaaha

zero / n. shunya

zigzag / adv. ghumaauro

zinc / n. jastaa

zone / n. anchal

zoo / n. chidiyaaghar

Also new From **HIPPOCRENE ...**

THE HIPPOCRENE COMPANION GUIDE TO SOUTHERN INDIA

Jack Adler

The Coromandel Coast boasts the second largest stretch of unbroken sandy beach in the world. The slopes of the Blue Mountains are lush with coffee, tea, and spice plantations. The peninsular states of Tamil Nadu, Andhra Pradesh, and Karnataka can be said to represent the essence of India.

From bustling cities to temple towns, palm-fringed beaches to hill stations, this comprehensive guide describes the attractions of each state, and highlights the former Portuguese colony of Goa, a natural gateway to the south. Packed with practical information and advice, it discusses discount travel passes, shopping, cuisine, the social and political scene, health and security, and the lilting India English language. Background material covers history, religion, and the arts, and there are suggestions on how to make contact with unusually friendly people.

Jack Adler, a travel writer for the Los Angeles Times, is author of *Travel Safety, Security Safeguards at Home and Abroad*, also published by Hippocrene Books.

252 pages, 5 1/2" x 8 1/2"
0632
ISBN 0-87052-030-X
$14.95 paperback

ENGLISH-HINDI STANDARD DICTIONARY

15,000 entries, modern colloquial and professional usage.

345 pages, 4 3/8" x 7"
0923
ISBN 0-87052-978-1
$11.95 paperback

HIPPOCRENE MASTER SERIES

This teach-yourself language series, now available in six languages, is perfect for the serious traveler, student or businessman. Imaginative, practical exercises in grammar are accompanied by cassette tapes for conversation practice. Available as a book/cassette package.

MASTERING FRENCH

0746	ISBN 0-87052-055-5	$11.95 BOOK
1003	ISBN 0-87052-060-1	$12.95 2 CASETTES
1085	ISBN 0-87052-136-5	$24.90 PACKAGE

MASTERING GERMAN

0754	ISBN 0-87052-056-3	$11.95 BOOK
1006	ISBN 0-87052-061-X	$12.95 2 CASSETTES
1087	ISBN 0-87052-137-3	$24.90 PACKAGE

MASTERING ITALIAN

0758	ISBN 0-87052-057-1	$11.95 BOOK
1007	ISBN 0-87052-066-0	$12.95 2 CASSETTES
1088	ISBN 0-87052-138-1	$24.90 PACKAGE

MASTERING SPANISH

0759	ISBN 0-87052-059-8	$11.95 BOOK
1008	ISBN 0-87052-067-9	$12.95 2 CASSETTES
1097	ISBN 0-87052-139-X	$24.90 PACKAGE

MASTERING ARABIC

0501	ISBN 0-87052-922-6	$14.95 BOOK
0931	ISBN 0-87052-984-6	$12.95 2 CASSETTES
1101	ISBN 0-87052-140-3	$27.90 PACKAGE

MASTERING JAPANESE

0748	ISBN 0-87052-923-4	$14.95 BOOK
0932	ISBN 0-87052-938-8	$12.95 2 CASSETTES
1102	ISBN 0-87052-141-1	$27.90 PACKAGE

Ask for these and other Hippocrene titles
at your local bookseller!